**W9-ASC-753**

# DRUG DANGERS

# The Dangers of E-Cigarettes

Peggy J. Parks

ReferencePoint
Press®

San Diego, CA

**About the Author**

Peggy J. Parks holds a bachelor of science degree from Aquinas College in Grand Rapids, Michigan, where she graduated magna cum laude. An author who has written dozens of educational books on a wide variety of topics for children and young adults, Parks lives in Muskegon, Michigan, a town that she says inspires her writing because of its location on the shores of Lake Michigan.

**For more information, contact:**
ReferencePoint Press, Inc.
PO Box 27779
San Diego, CA 92198
www. ReferencePointPress.com

LIBRARY OF CONGRESS CATALOGING-IN-PUBLICATION DATA

Names: Parks, Peggy J., 1951- author.
Title: The dangers of e-cigarettes / by Peggy J. Parks.
Description: San Diego, CA : ReferencePoint Press, Inc., 2017. | Series: Drug dangers | Includes bibliographical references and index.
Identifiers: LCCN 2016006624 (print) | LCCN 2016013819 (ebook) | ISBN 9781682820148 (hardback) | ISBN 9781682820155 (eBook)
Subjects: LCSH: Smoking--Juvenile literature. | Smoking--Health aspects--Juvenile literature. | Electronic cigarettes--Juvenile literature. | Teenagers--Tobacco use--Juvenile literature.
Classification: LCC HV5740 .P375 2017 (print) | LCC HV5740 (ebook) | DDC 362.29/6--dc23
LC record available at http://lccn.loc.gov/2016006624

# CONTENTS

**Chapter 1**                                    4
A Growing Trend

**Chapter 2**                                    16
What Are the Effects of E-Cigarettes?

**Chapter 3**                                    28
Are E-Cigarettes Addictive?

**Chapter 4**                                    40
What Risks Do E-Cigarettes Pose to Youth?

**Chapter 5**                                    52
How Should E-Cigarettes Be Regulated?

**Source Notes**                                 64

**Organizations to Contact**                     71

**For Further Research**                         75

**Index**                                        77

**Picture Credits**                              80

# CHAPTER 1: A Growing Trend

History is replete with stories of people whose dreams inspired them to create, invent, craft, and build. This was true of Hon Lik, a man from China for whom a dream was the motivating force behind a new kind of smoking device. At the time of his dream, Hon was working as a chemist at the Liaoning Provincial Institute of Traditional Chinese Medicine in northeastern China. He smoked two to three packs of cigarettes per day and wanted desperately to quit. Not only did he see how smoking was harming his health, he was also watching his father suffer from lung cancer after many years of heavy smoking.

One night, Hon had a terrifying dream that he was drowning in the sea. As he struggled helplessly and flailed about, water filled his lungs—then miraculously the water changed into a massive cloud of vapor and he could breathe again. Upon waking the next morning, Hon was convinced that the vapor cloud had some sort of meaning. On a notepad by his bedside, he scribbled a description of the strange dream so he would remember it. These hastily written notes would become the basis for a revolutionary product: an electronic cigarette (e-cigarette) that enables users to inhale liquid vapor rather than smoke. Hon patented his creation in 2003 and gave one of the first prototypes to his father, who used it until his death the following year. "It was too late for my father, but not for me,"[1] says Hon, who was able to give up traditional smoking after switching to e-cigarettes.

> "It was too late for my father, but not for me."[1]
>
> —Hon Lik, the inventor of e-cigarettes.

# No-Smoke Smoking

In the short time since Hon invented the e-cigarette, the device has evolved into an assortment of forms and sizes and is known by many different names. Along with e-cigarettes, they are also called vape pens, personal vaporizers, wands, hookah pens, and e-hookahs, as well as more formal names, such as electronic smoking devices and electronic nicotine delivery systems. Although the word *cigarette* is often used to describe the devices, nothing is burned, so there is no smoke. Rather, people who use e-cigarettes inhale and exhale an aerosol commonly called vapor, and the practice of doing so is known as vaping.

E-cigarettes differ widely in appearance, as NBC News correspondent Keith Wagstaff explains: "Some of them look like normal cigarettes, others like the Sonic Screwdriver from 'Doctor Who.'"[2] Despite the wide variety, the devices all have three

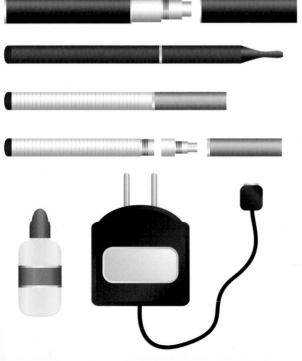

*This electronic cigarette kit contains a charger, liquid, and e-cigarettes that resemble traditional cigarettes. These models are frequently used by people who are new to vaping and prefer e-cigarettes that are a familiar size and shape.*

basic components: a lithium battery; a cartridge that holds liquid; and an atomizer, which is a vaporization chamber with a heating coil. E-cigarettes that resemble traditional cigarettes, such as the popular brands blu, Vuse, and Njoy, among others, are known as cigalikes or minis. These are often used by people who are new to vaping and are most comfortable with e-cigarettes that are a familiar size and shape. Cigalike cartridges are disposable; they come prefilled and must be replaced when empty. Advanced personal vaporizers, also known as vape pens, are considered mid-sized e-cigarettes. They are similar in size and shape to a fountain pen or cigar and are refillable. Vape mods, so named because of their modification capabilities, are bigger and more powerful e-cigarette models that often produce a high volume of vapor.

When an e-cigarette user inhales, the battery powers the atomizer heating coil to heat liquid (called e-liquid or e-juice) to the point of becoming an aerosol. The liquid is made up of water and compounds such as vegetable glycerin and propylene glycol, both of which are common additives in different foods and types of drugs. Also contained in e-liquid are flavorings, either natural or artificial, which are available in a staggering array of choices. As of January 2016 vaping enthusiasts could choose from more than seven thousand flavors ranging from traditional tobacco and menthol to chocolate malt, cappuccino, banana cream, bubble gum, raspberry, caramel, sour apple, and pomegranate. Britt E. Erickson, senior editor of the trade journal *Chemical & Engineering News*, adds: "Melon head, razzletaz, serious kiwi, Swedish fish, gummy bear, taste the rainbow—the list goes on."[3] Most e-liquid also contains nicotine, a drug that is extracted from the leaves of a plant in the nightshade family called the *Nicotiana tabacum*, more commonly known as tobacco. E-cigarette users may choose from varying strengths of nicotine or opt for nicotine-free e-liquid.

## Soaring Growth

In 2007 a company called Ruyan, for whom Hon Lik worked, first introduced e-cigarettes in the United States. Since that time the popularity of vaping has soared, which has led to booming e-cigarette

# An Inventor Ahead of His Time

The Chinese chemist Hon Lik is often called the father of e-cigarettes because he created the vapor-style device that is used today. But forty years before Hon patented his invention, an American named Herbert A. Gilbert created his own design. A military veteran from Beaver Falls, Pennsylvania, Gilbert was a heavy smoker who (correctly) theorized that what made cigarettes so hazardous was combustion and the resulting fumes that smokers inhaled. "The problem, as I concluded, was that when you burned leaves and wood, even if you did it in your backyard, it yielded a result that no one wanted to take into their lungs," he says. Gilbert set out to devise a way to substitute warm, moist, flavored air for burning tobacco. He was convinced that a battery-powered heat source would make his concept work, and in August 1965 Gilbert patented what he called a "smokeless non-tobacco cigarette."

Gilbert says he built prototypes of his electric cigarette, but they were destroyed in a fire. As for why his invention was never produced, smoking was popular and widespread during the 1960s. Very little was known about its health effects, so there likely was no demand for an e-cigarette. "Timing can be everything," says Gilbert, "and I was ahead of my time." He adds, though, that anyone who looks at his patent can see that he laid the groundwork for today's e-cigarette: "It may be positioned differently, sized differently, controlled differently . . . but it still follows the road map set forth in my patent drawings."

Quoted in James Dunworth, "An Interview with the Inventor of the Electronic Cigarette, Herbert A. Gilbert," *Ashtray Blog*, E-Cigarette Direct, October 2, 2013. www.ecigarettedirect.co.uk.

sales. The speed at which this growth has occurred is astounding to health officials and regulators, as well as to analysts who study global industry. According to Bonnie Herzog, a managing director and senior analyst at Wells Fargo Securities, the total US market for vaping devices has steadily risen from $1.7 billion in 2013 to $2.5 billion in 2014 to $3.5 billion in 2015, and is expected to reach a staggering $10 billion by 2017. Although the e-cigarette market is still a fraction of the immense market for tobacco products, that is expected to shift in coming years. "It's game-changing," says Herzog. "I'm of the view that in the next decade consumption of these products will surpass consumption of tobacco cigs."[4]

As of January 2016 there were nearly five hundred different brands of e-cigarettes and e-liquid. Nearly all are made in China, but the number of American manufacturers is growing. This includes major tobacco companies such as Lorillard, Imperial, Altria, and R.J. Reynolds, which initially dismissed vaping as a fad. That perception changed drastically when corporate leaders saw how lucrative e-cigarette investments could be for them. "Tobacco companies recognize the potential of this growing market," says the World Lung Foundation, "and are investing heavily in e-cigarette brands."[5]

The extraordinary growth of the e-cigarette industry is indicative of how popular vaping has become in recent years. A 2014 survey by the Centers for Disease Control and Prevention (CDC) showed that about 1 percent of American adults regularly used e-cigarettes in 2010. Within three years the number had grown to 2.6 percent. A summer 2015 poll for Reuters by the market research firm Ipsos found that about 10 percent of adults in the United States regularly practice vaping. That is almost four times higher than the amount reported in 2013 by the CDC's research.

This profoundly rapid growth is troubling to health officials for a number of reasons, such as the glaring lack of federal oversight. E-cigarettes are not regulated by the US Food and Drug Administration (FDA) as regular tobacco products are. Thus, there are no laws ensuring the purity or safety of e-cigarettes or e-liquid, nor are e-liquid manufacturers required to list ingredients on the bottles. Also, a great deal remains unknown about e-cigarettes and their effects on health. Although they are considered by many scientists to be safer than regular cigarettes, e-cigarettes have not been around long enough for researchers to study them in depth. "These products have not been thoroughly evaluated in scientific studies," says the National Institute on Drug Abuse (NIDA). "This may change in the near future, but for now, very little data exists on the safety of e-cigarettes."[6]

> "For now, very little data exists on the safety of e-cigarettes."[6]
>
> —NIDA, the United States' leading scientific research agency on drug abuse and addiction.

# Most Vapers Are Former Smokers

A 2015 CDC study shows that most people who use e-cigarettes are former or current smokers. This reinforces the widespread belief among scientists that many former smokers start vaping in an effort to quit smoking tobacco cigarettes.

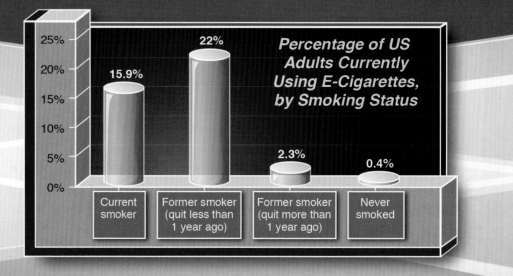

*Percentage of US Adults Currently Using E-Cigarettes, by Smoking Status*

- 15.9% — Current smoker
- 22% — Former smoker (quit less than 1 year ago)
- 2.3% — Former smoker (quit more than 1 year ago)
- 0.4% — Never smoked

Source: Charlotte A. Schoenborn and Renee M. Gindi, "Electronic Cigarette Use Among Adults: United States, 2014," *NCHS Data Brief*, October 2015. www.cdc.gov.

## From Smoking to Vaping

Numerous public surveys have been conducted, though, and offer clues about who is using e-cigarettes and why. Based on these surveys, health officials have learned that people of all ages and all walks of life have tried e-cigarettes. But as vaping's prevalence has steadily grown, it has become evident that the practice is most common among people who want to quit smoking tobacco cigarettes. During the summer 2015 Reuters/Ipsos poll, for example, more than 80 percent of current vapers were former smokers who either strongly agreed or somewhat agreed that e-smoking is a good way to help people quit smoking. This perception comes through in other surveys as well; when vapers are asked why they decided to start using e-cigarettes, the number one reason is the desire to quit smoking.

# E-Cigarettes and Tobacco Farming

The declining number of people who smoke traditional cigarettes has been good for public health but devastating for America's tobacco farmers. In Virginia, for instance, the number of tobacco farms dropped from 8,444 in 1992 to 558 in 2012; in South Carolina, tobacco farms shrank from 1,965 in 1992 to just 136 in 2012. E-cigarettes are soaring in popularity, however, and industry experts predict that the number of e-cigarette users will eventually surpass the number of traditional smokers. According to the online trade publication *Vaporizing Times*, this might actually be a blessing in disguise for tobacco farmers. This is because most e-liquid contains nicotine, which comes from cultivated tobacco plants. The author writes: "It's ironic to think that amid panic over the future of tobacco—reflected on stock markets around the world—that this new form of electronic smoking offers a potential revival for tobacco farmers."

As the popularity of e-cigarettes continues to grow, this will invariably lead to an increased demand for nicotine. Thus, it is conceivable that the demand for American tobacco will once again be on the rise. "Early signs are showing possible rejuvenation," the *Vaporizing Times* article states. "Electronic smoking poses no threat to tobacco farmers, to the contrary—it offers them a future."

*Vaporizing Times*, "E-Cigs: Blessing for Tobacco Industry?," October 15, 2014. https://vaporizingtimes.com.

Sarah Angst, who works at a vape shop in Lebanon, Missouri, started smoking when she was a teenager. After numerous unsuccessful attempts to quit smoking, she discovered something that finally worked: vaping. "It's becoming popular because it actually works to get people to quit smoking," says Angst. "Both me and my sister smoked since high school, and neither one of us could quit until we started vaping." Angst says that an important advantage of e-cigarettes for former smokers is that they can slowly lower the level of nicotine in the e-juice. She started out at the highest level of nicotine and has dropped to a fraction of that amount. "Customers will start out high," she says, "all of a sudden they're at the lowest level of nicotine that we have without even consciously trying to do that."[7]

To examine whether e-cigarettes help people stop smoking, researchers from KU Leuven, a university in Leuven, Belgium, conducted an eight-month study that was released in November 2014. Forty-eight people, all of whom were tobacco smokers with no interest in quitting, participated in the study. Depending on which group they were placed in, they either smoked e-cigarettes only or were allowed to smoke both tobacco cigarettes and e-cigarettes. By the end of the study, 21 percent of all participants had stopped smoking entirely, and an additional 23 percent reported cutting in half the number of tobacco cigarettes smoked per day. The researchers concluded that e-cigarettes had been just as effective at suppressing nicotine cravings as tobacco cigarettes. They contrast this with smokers who try to quit with no aids of any kind (using just willpower), of whom only about 5 percent remain smoke free. "With guidance on practical use, the nicotine e-cig offers many smokers a successful alternative for smoking less—or even quitting altogether," says study coauthor Frank Baeyens. "E-cig users get the experience of smoking a cigarette and inhale nicotine vapor, but do not suffer the damaging effects of a tobacco cigarette."[8]

## A Safer Alternative?

Despite such studies, health officials continue to discourage people from using e-cigarettes for smoking cessation. Yet this is highly controversial because smoking is such a deadly habit. Each year, nearly five hundred thousand Americans die from smoking-related illnesses, and smoking is the single largest cause of preventable death. Thus, scientists and health care practitioners often disagree about e-cigarettes. Many argue that the devices are far less harmful than smoking, can be effective as a smoking cessation tool, and could potentially save thousands of lives each year. "Obviously, it would be best if smokers could quit completely," says Michael Siegel, a professor at Boston University School of Public Health. "But if that's not possible, I think they'd be a lot better off with e-cigarettes. They're a safer alternative."[9] Siegel compares replacing traditional smoking with vaping to heroin users switching to the drug known as methadone. Although some view this as swapping one problem for another, methadone is much safer than heroin, and its use has saved innumerable lives.

Yet other health care professionals remain convinced that e-cigarettes should not be recommended for smoking cessation. Even if vaping does help people quit smoking, a great deal remains unknown about e-cigarette safety. "Are e-cigarettes better than the gums and the patches that are currently marketed as nicotine-replacement products? The answer is yes. They're about twice as good," says Robert Jackler, a Stanford University School of Medicine physician who specializes in otolaryngology (ear and throat). "But in reality, fewer than one in 10 adult smokers that adopt electronic cigarettes do so to actually eliminate smoking combustible cigarettes. Most of them continue to use both."[10] When people continue to smoke after they start vaping, scientists refer to this as dual use.

> "It would be best if smokers could quit completely. But if that's not possible, I think they'd be a lot better off with e-cigarettes. They're a safer alternative."[9]
>
> —Michael Siegel, a professor at Boston University School of Public Health.

Surveys have shown that Jackler is correct; many people do continue smoking after they start using e-cigarettes. But they do not necessarily plan to continue dual use. Many are in a state of transition, acclimating themselves to e-cigarettes with the goal of eventually cutting out regular smoking altogether. In the summer 2015 Ipsos/Reuters poll, 75 percent of dual users said they were smoking and vaping in an effort to quit smoking traditional cigarettes.

To examine the behaviors of dual users, researchers Jean-François Etter and Chris Bullen conducted a study and published it in February 2014. They surveyed 477 people on vaping and smoking cessation online forums and found that 22 percent of dual users had quit smoking tobacco cigarettes after a month of vaping. Of the remaining dual users, 46 percent had quit smoking after a year of vaping. Etter and Bullen concluded that e-cigarettes could contribute to smoking cessation in current smokers and help prevent relapse in former smokers.

*Many people who both use electronic cigarettes and smoke traditional cigarettes report that they use electronic cigarettes with the goal of eventually quitting regular smoking. Although some health professionals say that e-cigarettes are safer than traditional cigarettes, others argue that too little is known about the devices' safety.*

Bullen, along with researchers from Britain and New Zealand, conducted another 2014 study that also examined the effectiveness of e-cigarettes for smoking cessation. The researchers analyzed more than six hundred existing studies. They found that only thirteen of the studies were up to a level of quality known as the Cochrane standard, which recognizes the best science on a particular health-related subject. Of those, two were randomized control trials, which involve the most rigorous scientific experiments and are considered the gold standard of research. Based on their analysis, the researchers concluded that e-cigarettes could help people quit smoking or cut down on the number of cigarettes they smoked. They emphasize, however, that research is sparse and more studies are needed before such conclusions can be confirmed.

## Youth Vaping

As the popularity of e-cigarettes has spiked among Americans, vaping has caught on with young people as well as adults—and its prevalence is growing fast. The 2015 CDC National Youth

Tobacco Survey shows that current e-cigarette use among students in middle and high school tripled from 2013 to 2014. Vaping was most prevalent among high schoolers, rising from 4.5 percent of students in 2013 to 13.4 percent in 2014. That increase is especially dramatic when looking at numbers rather than percentages; the number of students who used e-cigarettes grew from 660,000 students in 2013 to 2 million in 2014. Among middle schoolers, current e-cigarette use rose from 1.1 percent (120,000 students) in 2013 to nearly 4 percent (450,000 students) in 2014. "This is a really bad thing," says CDC director Thomas R. Frieden. He emphasizes that teenagers' brains are not yet fully developed, and research has shown that nicotine harms the developing brain. "This is another generation being hooked by the tobacco industry. It makes me angry."[11]

> "This is another generation being hooked by the tobacco industry. It makes me angry."[11]
>
> —Thomas R. Frieden, director of the CDC.

The CDC survey also revealed that as vaping's prevalence grew among teens, traditional smoking plummeted. According to some analysts, this could suggest that teens who smoke may be using e-cigarettes as a way to quit smoking. Gregory Conley, president of the industry group American Vaping Association, points out that the drop in teen smoking is an incredibly positive development, one that is not being emphasized enough. "What you're seeing is the largest decline in teen smoking in the history of the [youth tobacco] study," says Conley. "It occurs at the same time as this dramatic increase of experimentation of vaping."[12]

In Westchester County, New York, teens who were interviewed for an April 2015 *New York Times* story say that many students at their high schools vape. Many started using e-cigarettes to kick a smoking habit. This was true of a Westchester teen named Tom, who says, "It's the healthy alternative taking over my school."[13] Tom estimates that about 70 percent of his friends practice vaping.

In 2015 a group of researchers from Yale University School of Medicine set out to learn what attracted so many young people to vaping. During interviews with more than five thousand Connecticut teens, the researchers asked what they found appealing about e-cigarettes. The top two answers were the different flavors of the e-liquids and the ability to do smoke (vapor) tricks such as blowing smoke rings or creating funnels of smoke that resemble miniature tornadoes. "We expected the flavors were attractive," says Yale researcher Suchitra Krishnan-Sarin. "But smoke tricks were a surprise to us."[14]

## The Potential for Good, the Potential for Harm

E-cigarettes are a relatively new product, and much remains unknown about them. Yet this uncertainty has not stopped people of all ages and walks of life from vaping. Health care practitioners do not always agree on whether e-cigarettes should be used as a smoking cessation aid. Health officials worry most about vaping's growing popularity among young people and the possible implications for their long-term health. Yet even this is speculative, since e-cigarettes are too new for any long-term health studies to be conducted. This was reflected in a 2014 statement by Mitch Zeller, who directs the FDA's Center for Tobacco Products. Speaking to a congressional panel, Zeller emphasized that there was little scientific evidence about e-cigarettes. Therefore, all he could comfortably say was, "They have the potential to do good; they have the potential to do harm."[15]

# CHAPTER 2: What Are the Effects of E-Cigarettes?

**A**s health officials have observed vaping's soaring popularity, they have become increasingly alarmed about its potential health hazards. Although most scientists agree that e-cigarettes are less harmful than tobacco cigarettes, and many support using e-cigarettes as a tool to quit smoking, vaping remains mired in uncertainty. "In general," says the American Heart Association, "the health effects of e-cigarettes have not been well studied, and the potential harm incurred by long-term use of these devices remains completely unknown."[16] Because definitive answers about vaping's health effects are sorely needed, e-cigarette research is a high priority.

Despite the lack of conclusive evidence, the public largely regards vaping as unsafe. This was revealed during an October 2015 poll by the Harvard T.H. Chan School of Public Health and STAT. The poll found that 65 percent of adults believe e-cigarettes can harm the health of people who use them. In addition, nearly half of respondents thought the sale of flavored nicotine cartridges should be prohibited to people of any age. Such negative attitudes toward e-cigarettes and vaping surprised the researchers who conducted the poll. Survey director Robert Blendon, a Harvard professor of health policy and political analysis, explains: "For a new product . . . you wouldn't have expected that people would have reached as firm a judgment about this as they have." Particularly surprising, says Blendon, was that people's responses were "nearly identical to what you find asking about tobacco cigarettes."[17]

## Conflicting Perspectives

The widespread public perception that e-cigarettes are harmful is a source of contention for vaping enthusiasts and those who represent the vaping industry. They argue that the concerns are alarmist and overblown, based on subjective opinion more than fact. Those who are able to quit smoking tobacco cigarettes after switching to e-cigarettes are especially vocal about the issue because they think their lives have changed for the better.

This is the case for Jason, a man from Louisville, Colorado, who is a partner in a vaping and e-liquid manufacturing business. Once a regular smoker, Jason has switched to vaping and now uses only zero-nicotine e-liquid. He is convinced that vaping can be enormously beneficial to public health. "We've been dismayed to see it take a pretty stern beating in the public arena," he says. One of Jason's biggest annoyances is the oft-repeated claim that no one knows exactly what is contained in e-liquid. Although that may be true of some suppliers, it is not true of all, including his business. "I am responsible for every bottle of e-liquid that leaves one of our wholesale customers' shelves," he says, "and I make 95 percent of it myself by hand. There are only four ingredients, and we did not find a single one of them on the surface of the Moon."[18]

The public's negativity toward vaping is also exasperating for Jacob Grier, a writer and vaping enthusiast from Portland, Oregon. He is frustrated by the fact that studies about vaping get a lot of publicity, even when they are not necessarily conclusive. "Despite alarmist speculations about trace chemicals found in e-cigarette vapor," says Grier, "the blunt fact of the matter is that there is no evidence that it poses any real danger." Grier believes that health officials and others who believe vaping is harmful are far too eager to restrict or ban e-cigarettes without having all the facts. "They'll be the first to tell you that more study of e-cigarettes is needed," says Grier. "But why wait for results? They're ready to ban first and ask questions later."[19]

> "Despite alarmist speculations about trace chemicals found in e-cigarette vapor, the blunt fact of the matter is that there is no evidence that it poses any real danger."[19]
>
> —Jacob Grier, a writer and vaping enthusiast from Portland, Oregon.

*A woman exhales vapor from an e-cigarette. The growing popularity of vaping concerns many health professionals, who insist that the safety of e-cigarettes is as yet unproven.*

## *Safer* Does Not Mean *Safe*

Health officials do not deny that much remains unknown about e-cigarettes. Researchers have been studying the devices for only a short time, and their concerns are often based on speculation about what *might* happen. But many say that this uncertainty alone is cause for alarm. With so many unanswered questions about vaping, health officials fear that its explosive popularity could lead to a public health crisis.

Brett Belchetz, an emergency room physician from Toronto, Canada, is baffled and dismayed that people would vape without knowing what it might do to them. He says:

> It's stunning that so many are willing to inhale from an e-cigarette, taking into their lungs an unknown, potentially toxic mix of chemical vapour, solely because an e-cigarette marketer tells them it's safe to do so.

In an era where so many decry the use of genetically modified grain, panic over the use of pesticides in fruit and vegetable production, and are willing to change their entire diet over the mere unproven suggestion that gluten might be bad for their digestive tract, why would they risk e-cigarettes?[20]

Avrum Spira, a pulmonologist (lung specialist) with Boston University School of Medicine, is adamant that the public needs to understand the possible risks of inhaling from e-cigarettes. As someone who has treated numerous patients for smoking-related lung diseases, including cancer, Spira does not want mistakes of the past to be repeated. He says that after tobacco cigarettes became popular among Americans, decades passed before research conclusively proved how deadly smoking is. Since the 1960s more than 20 million people in the United States have died from smoking-related causes. "We don't want to go down the road we did with cigarette smoking,"[21] he says.

Although Spira has seen firsthand the suffering caused by lung cancer and other respiratory diseases, he also readily acknowledges that e-cigarettes are not the same as tobacco cigarettes. "They don't have a lot of the components found in tobacco," he says. He adds, however: "They may be safer, but they may not be safe." People often confuse "safer than tobacco" with "safe," and Spira says it is crucial for the public to understand that these are two different things. "Even if e-cigarettes are not as bad as tobacco, it's important that we know what their health impacts are."[22]

> "Even if e-cigarettes are not as bad as tobacco, it's important that we know what their health impacts are."[22]
>
> —Avrum Spira, a pulmonologist (lung specialist) with Boston University School of Medicine.

# Vapor and the Lungs

A major research priority for Spira and other scientists is to learn more about how breathing e-cigarette vapor affects the lungs. What e-cigarette proponents call vapor is actually aerosol, a mass of tiny liquid and/or solid particles suspended in the air, like fog. Research has shown that when someone inhales vapor from an e-cigarette, most of the particles settle in the upper respiratory tract and the rest travel into the deepest part of the lungs. There the microscopic particles can become embedded in tiny sacs in lung tissue known as alveoli, where oxygen and carbon dioxide are exchanged. During a 2014 study at the North Carolina research institute RTI International, researchers concluded that about 40 percent of particles reach the alveoli. If any of those contain toxic substances, this can lead to damage throughout the lungs.

The potential for lung damage is one of scientists' biggest fears regarding the flavorings and additives (such as propylene glycol) contained in e-liquid. The FDA has designated these substances as "generally recognized as safe" (GRAS), but that applies only to eating them in food. According to Jonathan Foulds, professor of public health sciences and psychiatry at Penn State University's College of Medicine and Cancer Institute, breathing the substances in aerosol form is a very different matter. "We're putting things in e-cigs proven safe in foods, but it's not the same as putting it into a vapor and inhaling it," says Foulds. "A Mars bar is safe to eat, but I wouldn't want to inhale it. If something is safe as a food, it's not highly harmful, but we don't know what happens when you inhale it."[23]

> "We're putting things in e-cigs proven safe in foods, but it's not the same as putting it into a vapor and inhaling it. A Mars bar is safe to eat, but I wouldn't want to inhale it."[23]
>
> —Jonathan Foulds, a professor of public health sciences and psychiatry at Penn State University's College of Medicine and Cancer Institute.

One focus of e-cigarette vapor research is to examine what happens to e-liquid when it is heated. According to Spira, at high enough temperatures, the composition of the liquid changes. This causes new chemicals to form, and these are inhaled as vapor. "The question is: are those other chemicals harmful or not?,"[24] says Spira. According to a study published in the *New England Journal of Medicine*, one of those chemicals is formaldehyde, which is a known carcinogen (cancer-causing substance).

*E-cigarettes create vapor when the e-liquid they contain is heated. Studies have shown that this process changes the composition of the liquid, causing new chemicals to form that may be harmful. Here, a user fills an e-cigarette with liquid.*

The study was conducted in late 2014 by researchers from Portland State University in Oregon. They used a tank system e-cigarette, which is a large device with a variable-voltage battery, and heated e-liquid to various temperatures. After analyzing the resulting vapor to determine its chemical makeup, the researchers found an extremely high concentration of formaldehyde—up to fifteen times more than what is contained in tobacco cigarette smoke. "I think this is just one more piece of evidence amid a number of pieces of evidence that e-cigarettes are not absolutely safe,"[25] says David Peyton, a Portland State chemistry professor who was part of the research.

The vaping community was quick to denounce the study. Peyton and the other researchers detected formaldehyde only when the voltage was turned to its highest setting, and not at lower settings. So, according to vaping proponents, the findings were unrealistic because no one would ever crank up the voltage to such a high level. "If you hold the button on an e-cigarette for 100 seconds, you could potentially produce 100 times more formaldehyde

# Exploding E-Cigs

Several government agencies have researched e-cigarettes, but one agency's research is quite different from the rest. The US Fire Administration has investigated a rare occurrence: explosions and fires caused by e-cigarettes. At the time the agency's investigation was conducted, twenty-five incidents had been reported from 2009 to 2014. Most of these occurred while the device's lithium batteries were charging, but on two occasions people were vaping at the time. One man was hospitalized for eight days after an e-cigarette exploded in his face, sending burning debris and battery acid into his mouth, face, and eyes. The other incident was equally serious; an e-cigarette explosion caused severe burns, lost teeth, and partial loss of the victim's tongue.

In October 2015 a twenty-three-year-old man from Bakersfield, California, was seriously injured when an e-cigarette blew up while he was vaping. "It exploded in my face," says Vicente Garza. "I never thought something like this could happen." He suffered severe burns to his mouth and tongue, and his left index finger was so badly injured that doctors had to amputate it at the knuckle. After such a frightening experience, Garza quit vaping. "It's not something to play around with."

Quoted in CBS Los Angeles, "Bakersfield Man Suffers Serious Injuries After E-Cigarette Explosion," November 19, 2015. http://losangeles.cbslocal.com.

than you would ever get from a cigarette," says Gregory Conley, president of the American Vaping Association. "But no human vaper would ever vape at that condition, because within one second their lungs would be incredibly uncomfortable." That, Conley says, is because the vapor would be too hot and would taste bad, which he illustrates with an analogy of an overcooked steak. "I can take a steak and I can cook it on the grill for the next 18 hours, and that steak will be absolutely chock-full of carcinogens," he says. "But the steak will also be charcoal, so no one will eat it."[26]

## Hints of Cancer Risk

Spira's research has also focused on e-cigarette vapor. In fact, he was one of the first researchers to be awarded FDA funding to study the health consequences of vaping. His approach is to evaluate e-cigarettes based on his prior research with tobacco cigarettes. This has involved identifying certain genomic factors that could increase someone's risk for lung disease. The question, according to Spira, is: "Does exposure to e-cigarettes create the same genomic changes in the airway as tobacco cigarettes do?"[27]

One of Spira's research projects involved culturing a batch of human bronchial cells in liquid solution that contained, as he explains, "everything that comes out of an e-cigarette. The idea is that you're 'smoking the cells.'" Another batch of bronchial cells was grown in solution that contained the contents of tobacco smoke. Spira and his colleagues discovered that the two batches of cells showed similar genetic activity that could cause mutations that lead to cancer. "We found that the electronic cigarette was able to cause cells to become more cancer-like—they grew more quickly than a cell should be able to," says Spira. "That is one of the things that cancer cells do." He goes on to say that although this was a disturbing finding, it would be premature to declare that vaping can cause cancer. "We can't say that based on this data," says Spira. "What we're saying is that we have evidence from cells in culture that e-cigarettes could have effects that are similar to tobacco smoking and that many more studies are needed before we can say this is a much safer product."[28]

## Butter-Flavored Danger

As researchers have continued to study the effects of e-cigarettes, they have become increasingly concerned about a chemical known as diacetyl. A by-product of fermentation, diacetyl is found naturally in butter, cheese, beer, wine, and some other foods. For the purpose of replicating diacetyl's creamy, buttery taste, scientists in the mid-twentieth century created a synthetic form of diacetyl. The chemical is commonly added to margarine, baked goods such as cakes and cookies, candy, ice cream, and snack foods such as pretzels, chips, and microwave popcorn. Like many other substances, diacetyl (whether natural or synthetic) is not harmful when eaten. When heated and inhaled, however, it

*A large percentage of e-cigarettes and e-liquids contain diacetyl, a flavoring chemical that is added to many products, including microwave popcorn. Because diacetyl can cause a lung-destroying disease called bronchiolitis obliterans when heated and inhaled, its presence in these products has potentially dire health consequences for e-cigarette users.*

can lead to development of a respiratory disease known as bronchiolitis obliterans, which destroys lung tissue.

Bronchiolitis obliterans is colloquially known as "popcorn lung disease." This is because it was first discovered in workers at the Gilster-Mary Lee microwave popcorn factory in Jasper, Missouri. In 2000 the National Institute for Occupational Safety and Health investigated reports of abnormally high rates of respiratory illness among the plant's employees. Investigators found that a large percentage of workers suffered from chronic cough and shortness of breath, as well as more serious respiratory problems such as chronic bronchitis and asthma. By 2002 the investigators had determined that eight Gilster-Mary Lee workers suffered from bronchiolitis obliterans as the result of repetitively inhaling diacetyl in the course of their jobs. Half of them needed lung transplants, and in the years since, five of the workers have died of respiratory causes.

In December 2015 researchers from the Harvard T.H. Chan School of Public Health released a study with disturbing findings about diacetyl. Analysis of fifty-one types of flavored e-cigarettes and e-liquid found that the chemical was contained in more than 75 percent of the samples. Because there are no federal regulations about e-liquid labeling, customers have no way of knowing if diacetyl is in the bottles they purchase. Says lead study author Joseph Allen, "Diacetyl and other related flavoring chemicals are used in many other flavors behind butter-flavored popcorn, including fruit flavors, alcohol flavors, and, we learned in our study, candy-flavored e-cigarettes."[29]

The concern over diacetyl in e-liquid prompted a Milwaukee, Wisconsin, newspaper to conduct its own investigation. In October 2015 representatives from the *Milwaukee Journal Sentinel* visited vape shops throughout Milwaukee and purchased five bottles of top-selling brands of e-liquid. The samples were analyzed by researchers from Marquette University, and all five were determined to contain diacetyl. Another discovery was that the method the vaping industry typically uses to analyze e-liquids is not sensitive enough to detect potentially harmful levels of diacetyl. "As a result," says an October 2015 account of the investigation, "e-liquid makers across the country claim their formulas are diacetyl free when sometimes they are not."[30]

## Secondhand Vapor

Many people who start using e-cigarettes only vape outside or in places where smoking is typically allowed. But health officials are aware of numerous reports of people using e-cigarettes indoors and in smoke-free public spaces, and this has become a concern. As with e-cigarettes themselves, little is known about whether secondhand vapor is harmful. The American Lung Association cites two studies that found the cancer-causing chemicals formaldehyde, benzene, and tobacco-specific nitrosamines in secondhand e-cigarette emissions. There is, however, no evidence definitively showing that e-cigarette emissions are unsafe for anyone to inhale.

Research by Suzaynn Schick, a professor at the University of California–San Francisco, focuses on secondhand vapor. She also studies what she calls "third-hand" vapor, or what happens to the nicotine in e-cigarettes after it has been exhaled and lands on surfaces. "I know that when you release nicotine into the room and it settles on a surface, it reacts with normal gases in the air to form carcinogens," says Schick. Her research focuses on the potential health consequences of e-cigarette vapor to nonusers. Specifically, she is concerned about particles in the vapor, as she explains: "The reason I care about particles is that breathing particles causes cardiovascular disease, causes people to die of heart attacks, plain and simple."[31]

## Tiny Bottles, Big Worries

Another emerging problem is e-liquid itself, primarily because of its nicotine content. In concentrated liquid form, nicotine is potent and powerful. According to the American Association of Poison Control Centers (AAPCC), one teaspoon of liquid nicotine is enough to kill a child, and even smaller amounts can cause serious illness.

In fact, throughout the United States, there has been a huge increase in calls to poison control centers about liquid nicotine exposure. The term *exposure* means that someone has had contact with liquid nicotine. For example, the substance may have been ingested, inhaled, absorbed by the skin, or spilled into the eyes. The AAPCC, which maintains the only poisoning surveillance database in the country, reports that in 2012 there were 460 of these kinds of calls to poison control centers. By the end of 2014 the number had jumped to 3,783—more than a 700 percent increase in two years. Slightly more than half of the poison-related calls were about young children under age six. "It's not a matter of if a child will be poisoned or killed," says Lee Cantrell, director of the San Diego division of the California Poison Control System. "It's a matter of when."[32] Less than a year after Cantrell's prediction, it tragically came true.

In December 2014 a toddler from Fort Plain, New York, died after consuming e-liquid. Eli James "EJ" Hotaling, who was eighteen months old, discovered a bottle of e-liquid on a low table and drank it. He began having convulsions and was rushed to

# Vaping and Oral Health

As a health care professional, Mark Burhenne is well aware of the controversy over vaping, and he sees both sides of the issue. He acknowledges that e-cigarettes have not been fully studied and that much remains to be learned about them. But Burhenne is a dentist, so he does know what vaping can do to teeth and gums. "I can say that e-cigarettes can still cause gum recession and other oral health problems because they still deliver nicotine, even if it's in smaller doses than traditional cigarettes."

Nicotine is a vasoconstrictor, meaning it reduces (constricts) normal blood flow through the veins. According to Burhenne, insufficient blood flow impedes gums from getting enough oxygen and nutrients to stay healthy. "Nicotine chokes tissues in the mouth from the blood it needs to survive," he says, "causing death of the gum tissues." This can lead to gum disease, which is an inflammation of the gum line that can progress to affect bones that surround and support the teeth. Also, says Burhenne, this restricted blood flow can impede the body's ability to produce saliva, which can cause a buildup of bacteria, dry mouth, and tooth decay. Burhenne's advice for those who vape is to watch for signs of gum disease, such as bleeding or receding gums, but if possible to quit entirely.

Mark Burhenne, "No Smoke, but Plenty of Fire: How Do E-Cigarettes Affect Oral Health?," Ask the Dentist, January 19, 2015. http://askthedentist.com.

the hospital, where he was pronounced dead. The cause of EJ's death was later determined to be cardiac arrhythmia from nicotine poisoning.

## Time Will Tell

E-cigarettes have not been around very long, but they are already the subject of massive controversy. Very little is known about their effects, and virtually nothing is known about how vaping might affect people over the long term. Scientists are convinced that there is reason to be concerned about e-cigarette use, and they are aggressively pursuing research to learn more. Vaping supporters argue that study findings have been inconclusive and health officials' negativity toward e-cigarettes is misguided and alarmist. As research continues, there will hopefully be less controversy and more certainty.

# CHAPTER 3: Are E-Cigarettes Addictive?

The addictive nature of tobacco cigarettes is widely recognized and has been for years. That is largely because among the thousands of chemicals contained in tobacco smoke is nicotine, which is a powerful addictive drug. "It's likely the most addicting chemical in common human exposure," says Winona, Minnesota, physician Frank Bures. "It is said to be 1,000 times more addictive than alcohol, 10 to 100 more times than barbiturates (rarely used today), and 5 to 10 more times than morphine or cocaine."[33]

Scientists are only beginning to study the effects of vaping, so little is known about its potential for addiction. Many believe vaping can be addictive, though, as cancer specialist and Humana chief medical officer Roy A. Beveridge explains: "It's important to note that the same addictive chemical found in e-cigarettes and cigarettes is nicotine, which causes addiction to smoking." That factor alone, according to Beveridge, raises crucial questions such as: "Are people using e-cigarettes to just continue smoking in a different way? Is it a transfer of one addiction to another?"[34] As important as these questions are, the answers remain elusive.

## What Vapers Say

The American public, including many who use e-cigarettes, leans toward believing that vaping is addictive. During the summer 2015 Reuters/Ipsos poll, participants were asked to agree or disagree with a number of statements, one of which said that people can become addicted to e-smoking. Of nearly six thousand adults who participated, 60 percent either strongly agreed or agreed that people could become addicted. Surprisingly, most of the e-cigarette users who took part in the survey were even more convinced that vaping was addictive. Of the 465 adults surveyed who were current vapers, 70 percent either strongly agreed or agreed that people could become addicted to e-cigarettes.

John Dunn, a man in his mid-thirties from Garland, Texas, is convinced that vaping is addictive. Dunn was able to quit smoking after he started vaping, and several of his friends did as well. But some of them got addicted to e-cigarettes. "I've seen people get on the vapors and not be able to stop," he says. Dunn would like to see warning labels on e-cigarette products because it would help people be more informed. "They should know they might get addicted,"[35] he says.

Rachael Lloyd is also convinced that e-cigarettes are addictive because of what she personally experienced. In 2012 when Lloyd took her first puff of an e-cigarette, she thought she had discovered a miracle. At the time she was smoking a pack of Marlboro Lights per day, and she was delighted to discover that vaping did not bother her lungs. "I was struck by how lovely it felt to breathe so deeply," she says. Soon after that Lloyd went through a particularly difficult time and began vaping more often—and more habitually. "I began to question the extent of my vaping," says Lloyd, who was at one point vaping up to forty times per day. If she left home without her vaping paraphernalia, she would "fly into a panic" and immediately find a source to buy what she needed. "I couldn't function properly without my new prop," she says, "and my dependence increased." Finally, Lloyd talked to her doctor, who shocked her by saying that forty inhalations of vapor per day was equivalent to forty cigarettes in terms of nicotine. "There was no doubt about it, I was a vape addict,"[36] she says. With her doctor's help, she gave up e-cigarettes and plans to never use them again.

Nick Green's experience with e-cigarettes could not have been more different, however. "Electronic cigarettes and 'vaping' have changed my life," he says. A former habitual smoker, Green discovered vaping in 2009 and was astounded at how easily he was

> "It's important to note that the same addictive chemical found in e-cigarettes and cigarettes is nicotine, which causes addiction to smoking."[34]
>
> —Cancer specialist and Humana chief medical officer Roy A. Beveridge.

able to quit smoking. Immediately, he started blogging and creating YouTube videos to tell the world about e-cigarettes. "People needed to know about this miracle device," he says. "They needed to know that a staunch tobacco lover had just effortlessly gone three full days without a cigarette. I had to tell people, as many as I could." In the years since he first discovered vaping, Green has personally spoken with long-time smokers who were able to finally kick the habit only because of e-cigarettes. "Non-smokers may never understand how truly difficult it is to stop using cigarettes," he says. "I think that if they did, then no one would stand between smokers and their ability to purchase and use electronic cigarettes."[37]

## Addiction and Brain Chemistry

Although e-cigarette research is still very young, scientists have studied the brain and addiction for decades. In the process, they have learned a great deal about what addiction is, the factors that contribute to it, and how it develops. Unlike years ago, when addiction of any kind was viewed as a personal weakness or moral failing, scientists today know better. Referring to "powerful myths and misconceptions about the nature of addiction," NIDA director Nora D. Volkow writes: "When scientists began to study addictive behavior in the 1930s, people addicted to drugs were thought to be morally flawed and lacking in willpower. . . . Today, thanks to science, our views and our responses to addiction and other substance use disorders have changed dramatically." According to Volkow, scientists' improved understanding of the brain has vastly expanded their knowledge of how different drugs affect the brain, as well as how addiction develops. "As a result of scientific research," she says, "we know that addiction is a disease that affects both the brain and behavior."[38]

> "People needed to know about this miracle device. They needed to know that a staunch tobacco lover had just effortlessly gone three full days without a cigarette."[37]
>
> —Nick Green, a former habitual smoker who was able to quit after discovering vaping in 2009.

Understanding addiction begins with knowing something about the function of brain chemistry. The most powerful, complex organ in the human body, the brain is composed of an intricate network of nerve cells known as neurons. These cells are constantly communicating with each other, sending and receiving messages in the form of rapid-fire electrochemical signals. The well-orchestrated process is made possible by brain chemicals known as neurotransmitters, which facilitate the transfer of signals from one neuron to another across tiny gaps known as synapses. For each neurotransmitter there is a receiving neuron called a receptor. "A neurotransmitter and its receptor operate like a 'key and lock,'" says NIDA, "an exquisitely specific mechanism that ensures that each receptor will forward the appropriate message only after interacting with the right kind of neurotransmitter."[39]

# The Way Nicotine Tricks the Brain

The neurotransmitter that is most affected by nicotine is known as acetylcholine. Its receptors are located throughout the body, including in the digestive system and body organs, but the most important are in the brain. Acetylcholine receptors are involved with respiration, heart rate, memory, alertness, and muscle movement. According to NIDA, when someone inhales nicotine, this disrupts the normal function of acetylcholine and its receptors. "Because nicotine is shaped similarly to acetylcholine," says NIDA, "it can fit in the same receptors and act just like acetylcholine."[40] In this way nicotine tricks receptors into thinking it is natural acetylcholine so they will bind to it.

After someone habitually uses nicotine over a period of time, there is increased activity at the receptors because they are being activated naturally (by acetylcholine) as well as artificially (by nicotine). "This change in balance causes the brain to 'think' there is too much acetylcholine," says NIDA, "and react by reducing the number of receptors and releasing less acetylcholine into the synapse." As a result of this increased chemical activity, the brain starts to need nicotine just to maintain its normal functioning. "These changes in the brain cause a nicotine user to feel abnormal when not using nicotine," says NIDA. "In order to feel normal,

This image depicts an acetylcholine receptor, a type of neuron in the human body that receives the neurotransmitter acetylcholine. Nicotine use interferes with normal acetylcholine receptor activity, resulting in the brain needing nicotine simply to function normally.

the user has to keep his or her body supplied with nicotine. This is addiction."[41]

Another effect of nicotine is the release of abnormally high levels of dopamine. A neurotransmitter that is often called the feel-good chemical, dopamine is involved in pleasure, arousal, and mood change, among other functions. When nicotine is released into the brain, this stimulates a circuit in the brain known as the reward system. People who smoke are not likely aware of the precise chemical reaction taking place in their brains. But because of how nicotine works, they will unconsciously want to smoke in order to maintain the high dopamine levels and the pleasurable feelings associated with the drug. Although scientists do not know if the same process will occur with e-cigarettes, it is enough of a concern to warrant extensive research.

## E-Cigs and Nicotine

It is commonly believed that when people switch from tobacco cigarettes to e-cigarettes, they inhale less nicotine. This is hard to quantify, however, because there are so many variables. Research has shown that each time someone smokes a cigarette, he or she absorbs about 1 milligram of nicotine; thus, someone who smokes a pack of cigarettes per day will absorb 20 milligrams of

## Labels Can Deceive

E-cigarettes and e-liquid contain varying degrees of nicotine, which usually ranges in strength from 0 to 36 milligrams per milliliter (mg/ml). Consumers who buy these products can choose the level of nicotine they want—but according to a 2014 study, they may not be getting what they expect. The study was conducted by Skyler Reinhardt and Maciej Goniewicz from the Roswell Park Cancer Institute in Buffalo, New York, who tested thirty-two bottles of e-liquid they bought from online vendors. They found that one-quarter of the samples differed from the labeled nicotine content by at least 20 percent and in some cases by more than 100 percent. Moreover, all three bottles that were labeled "nicotine free" contained traceable amounts of the drug.

"E-cigarettes have enormous potential to hook all types of users," Reinhardt and Goniewicz state. "Nonsmokers that try e-cigarettes, even with nicotine-free refill solutions, may develop an addiction because of faulty manufacturing." They go on to say that for smokers who have turned to vaping as a way of giving up tobacco cigarettes, "there is a possibility that they are actually inhaling more nicotine than is labeled," which could undermine their attempts to cut back.

Quoted in Crystal Phend, "'Nicotine-Free' E-Cigs Still Deliver the Juice," MedPage Today, February 10, 2014. www.medpagetoday.com.

nicotine per day. But for a number of reasons, measurements of e-liquid nicotine are not as precise as those of cigarettes. Nicotine content varies based on factors such as how much is contained in e-cigarettes and/or e-liquid and how often the person vapes. Also, because e-cigarettes are not subject to government regulations, exactly how much nicotine is contained in a bottle of e-liquid is often unknown, despite what may be stated on a label. "The current state of the e-vapor business is rather chaotic," says reporter and vaping enthusiast Matt McConnell, "and there are so many types of e-cigs with such varying degrees of quality that performance cannot be narrowed down to a statistical constant."[42]

Mike Morgan, a forty-eight-year-old long-term smoker from Kentucky, quit smoking a pack of cigarettes a day after his moth-

*This display of electronic smoking materials includes bottles of e-liquids. Because the amount of nicotine contained in these liquids varies widely, it is difficult for researchers to determine how much nicotine electronic cigarettes deliver to the user compared to tobacco cigarettes.*

er died of lung cancer. Now he vapes from ten to fifteen times a day and describes vaping from the viewpoint of someone who has been addicted to nicotine for many years: "You don't get the great big burst of nicotine you get with a cigarette, but at this point, it satisfies my cravings."[43]

As researchers study the effects of e-cigarettes, several have delved into the devices' addictive potential. One such researcher is Jonathan Foulds, a professor of public health sciences and psychiatry at Penn State College of Medicine. For a study published in October 2014, Foulds explored how e-cigarettes may lead to dependence, and then compared that with dependence on tobacco cigarettes.

To gauge these levels of dependence, Foulds and his research team designed a comprehensive online survey. It included questions designed to assess previous dependence on cigarettes and nearly identical questions to assess current dependence on e-cigarettes. More than thirty-five hundred current vapers, who were all former smokers, took part in the study. Using a rating scale from 1 to 20, they answered questions about their past addiction to smoking and current e-cigarette dependence. The researchers concluded that people who had previously been addicted to smoking did not experience the same level of dependence on vaping. "We don't have long-term health data of e-cig use yet," says Foulds, "but any common sense analysis says that e-cigs are much less toxic. And our paper shows that they appear to be much less addictive, as well. So in both measures they seem to have advantages when you're concerned about health."[44]

## As Addictive as Cigarettes?

Other scientists studying the addictive potential of vaping have come to very different conclusions. One is Najat A. Saliba, a researcher from the American University of Beirut in Lebanon. In July 2015 Saliba and his colleagues published a study showing that vaping products with very high nicotine content could make quitting "particularly difficult should users decide to try."[45]

Saliba's research team tested commercially available samples of e-liquids to determine what type of nicotine each contained.

The type is important because not all nicotine is the same; some types are much more addictive than others. Protonated nicotine, for example, has not been enhanced with any additives. This is very different from freebase nicotine, which has been chemically altered to be more potent and more addictive. Also called "spiked" nicotine, freebase nicotine is more easily absorbed by the body and reaches the brain faster than protonated nicotine. Studies have consistently found that the majority of the nicotine in tobacco cigarettes is the freebase type.

Saliba and his colleagues found that freebase nicotine was the most common type used in vaping devices—which could mean that vaping is just as addictive as smoking tobacco. Another finding was that the concentration of nicotine as measured in vapor differed from sample to sample and often did not match what was printed on e-liquid bottle labels. In the published study, the researchers write: "These discrepancies may result from poor quality control at the manufacturing facility, from variations in label definitions across brands, or both."[46] They recommend that additional studies be conducted to further investigate their findings.

The addictive potential of e-cigarettes was also the focus of a 2015 study published in the journal *Tobacco Control*. The researchers found that vaping could be as addictive as smoking because of common additives known as pyrazines. Colloquially known as "Super Juice," pyrazines were created in the 1970s by the Philip Morris tobacco company to make low-tar or "light" cigarettes taste more like full-flavored cigarettes. The effects were more powerful than that, however; pyrazines actually enhanced cigarettes' addictiveness. During the 2015 study, the researchers discovered that the same pyrazines that had been added to cigarettes were also contained in e-liquid. Although the study did not conclusively prove that vaping was as addictive as smoking, the researchers offered a warning: "Pyrazines appear to increase product appeal and make it easier for non-smokers to initiate smoking, more difficult for current smokers to quit, much easier for former smokers to relapse into smoking, and may mask the risks of both active and passive smoking."[47]

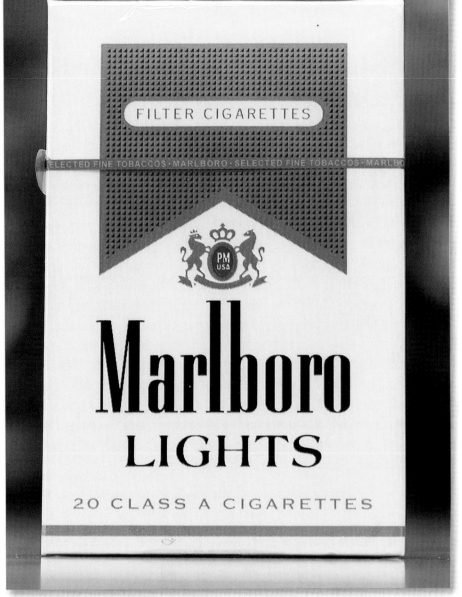

*So-called "light" cigarettes like the brand pictured here contain additives known as pyrazines that make them even more addictive than regular cigarettes. A 2015 study found that e-liquid also contains pyrazines, leading researchers to speculate that vaping may turn out to be as addictive as smoking traditional cigarettes.*

## The Challenges of Quitting

Because the vaping craze is still relatively new, there are no long-term studies on people who have been hooked on e-cigarettes and had trouble giving them up. This was one of the topics explored in the 2015 Reuters/Ipsos poll. Participants who said they

# Analyzing Brain Activity

For decades, scientists have studied addiction and how it affects the brain. Many questions remain unanswered about people's addiction to smoking, however; specifically, whether their addiction is fueled by more than just the nicotine in cigarettes. Matt Wall, an imaging scientist at Imperial College London in England, explains: "There's something unique about the drug (nicotine) and the delivery system—the smoking—combined which makes it really, really addictive." Functional magnetic resonance imaging (fMRI) technology, which detects activity in different regions of the brain by analyzing blood flow, would be an ideal way to study smoking's effect on the brain. But using fMRI while people are smoking cigarettes is neither feasible nor safe. So for a 2014 pilot study, Wall and his colleagues used fMRI technology while participants puffed on e-cigarettes. This was safe to do because the devices do not burn, and they emit only vapor.

The study was small, and the researchers were not able to draw any definitive conclusions. But they did observe activity in areas of the brain linked to reward and addiction, as well as areas involved in perception of taste and smell. This was intriguing enough to warrant further study. Wall plans to conduct additional research with vaping participants to learn more about the addiction potential of smoking and vaping and how they affect brain activity.

Quoted in Kate Kelland, "Studies of 'Vaping' Brain May Offer Clues on Smoking Addiction," Reuters, November 13, 2014. www.reuters.com.

regularly vaped were asked whether they had tried to quit using e-smoking devices, and 57 percent said they had. Members of the same group (currently using e-cigarettes) were asked if they considered themselves addicted to nicotine, and 68 percent answered yes.

Mandy Stadtmiller, a writer and editor from New York City, became addicted to vaping and had a very difficult time giving it up. Long before she tried vaping, she knew what addiction felt like because she had her first cigarette at age thirteen—and immediately felt stress leave her body. "I thought to myself (as most addicts do): 'No matter what comes, I will never give this up,'" she says. Throughout the following years, she smoked off and on and had her first try at vaping in 2012. She became hooked almost immediately. "I would sit and puff, sit and puff, write and puff, forever able to give myself a buzz of nicotine, nicotine, nicotine," Stadtmiller says. She soon noticed that vaping had the same hold on her as smoking once had. "It's the exact same bullying manner that real cigarettes control your life," she says. "You are forced to plan your activities around them, and you obsess as to when your next one will be. . . . You know it's going to be great, that's for sure. So when is it going to be? When is it going to be, when, when, when?"[48]

Stadtmiller had no doubt that she had to quit vaping. She reopened a book about addiction that she had previously found motivating and jotted its main principles down on a goal list. That became her blueprint for quitting, as she explains: "You develop a little 'outline' that you can remind yourself of when the desire rears itself." It took time and dedication, but the plan that Stadtmiller developed for herself began to work. "Will I smoke tonight? Tomorrow? This year? Ever again? I don't know," she says. "But I'm thrilled that this is working for now."[49]

> "I thought to myself (as most addicts do): 'No matter what comes, I will never give this up."[48]
>
> —Mandy Stadtmiller, a writer and editor from New York City.

## Questions Linger

Like other aspects of e-cigarettes, whether they are addictive has not been definitively proved. Based on decades of research, scientists have compiled a wealth of information about the brain and addiction, but they are only just beginning to study the addictive potential of vaping. Unlike cigarettes, there are many deviations in vaping devices, and their nicotine content is not always what e-cigarette users expect when they buy the products. Health officials hope that future research will yield more concrete data and clear up many of today's uncertainties.

# CHAPTER 4: What Risks Do E-Cigarettes Pose to Youth?

ameron Anderson was a junior in high school the first and only time she tried vaping. The school year was coming to an end, and Anderson was at a party with a bunch of other teens. She became intrigued by the vaping games many of them played, such as blowing out clouds of thick vapor that formed O shapes. "They looked like they were having a good time doing vape tricks together," says Anderson. Wanting to see for herself what vaping was like, she decided to try it, and at first she enjoyed it. "I really liked vaping at the time," she says, "because of the intimacy we all had while sharing this one vape."[50] The next day, however, she felt differently.

Anderson woke in the morning not feeling well; she suffered from chest pain and a sore throat. Those symptoms did not last long, but for about a month, whenever she laughed it came out as a wheeze. She says she promised herself she would never use e-cigarettes again, "in hopes that my laugh would return to normal so I didn't sound like a broken tuba."[51]

## Why Teens Vape

Anderson decided to try vaping for the same reason as many teens: because she was curious about it. That is characteristic of young people; by virtue of their age, they are often motivated to try new things out of curiosity. This came through clearly during a 2015 survey called Monitoring the Future (MTF), which involved nearly forty-five thousand eighth-, tenth-, and twelfth-grade students throughout the United States. Conducted each year on behalf of NIDA, the MTF was the first major study to ask American teens about e-cigarettes and vaping. Among those who vaped, more than half said they started doing it to experiment, just to see what it would be like. Other top reasons chosen by students were because the vapor tastes good, they were bored and had nothing else to do, they wanted to have a good time with their friends, they wanted to relax and feel relief from tension, and they think vaping looks cool (in that order).

Of particular interest to the MTF researchers was how few students said they vaped to quit smoking tobacco cigarettes. Although this is one of the primary reasons adults start using

*Young people enjoy themselves at a party. Those in this age group are often motivated to try new things, including vaping, out of curiosity. In one study, more than half of teens who had vaped had done so for this reason.*

e-cigarettes, it was low on the list of reasons teens gave. "Our finding that so few adolescents use e-cigarettes to stop smoking contrasts with studies of adults, who are more likely to use e-cigarettes to try to stop smoking cigarettes,"[52] says University of Michigan sociologist Richard Miech, who is a senior MTF investigator.

Perception of risk—or rather, lack thereof—is another reason teens are likely to try vaping. Nearly all young people know about the innumerable health risks of tobacco cigarettes; in the 2015 MTF survey, 63 percent of eighth graders, 73 percent of tenth graders, and 76 percent of twelfth graders associated great risk with regular smoking. But the same survey showed that many teens view e-cigarettes much differently. When asked how much risk they think people take by regularly using e-cigarettes, 19 percent of eighth graders believed vapers were taking great risk. Of tenth graders, 17 percent believed there was great risk in regular use of e-cigarettes, and 16 percent of twelfth graders felt that way. "Part of the reason for the popularity of . . . e-cigarettes is the perception that they do not harm health,"[53] says Miech.

> "Part of the reason for the popularity of . . . e-cigarettes is the perception that they do not harm health."[53]
>
> —University of Michigan sociologist Richard Miech.

## Teens Do What Other Teens Do

Young people are usually influenced by their social environment, from how they dress and talk to whether they use drugs and/or alcohol. The same is true of vaping, according to a 2014 study by researchers at the University of Southern California. They found a strong association between e-cigarette use among teens and psychosocial factors, such as home environment and friends' use of or attitudes toward e-cigarettes. For example, 34 percent of current teen e-cigarette users share a home with another e-cigarette user. In contrast, of all non-vaping teens, just 7.3 percent share a home with an e-cigarette user. Also among current e-cigarette users, nearly 50 percent had three or four friends who used

# Smoke Tricks and Cloud Competitions

Among the numerous surveys that have explored teen vaping is a December 2014 study by Yale School of Medicine psychiatry professor Suchitra Krishnan-Sarin. During eighteen focus groups with adolescents and young adults in Connecticut, she and fellow researchers led with a question: What is cool about e-cigarettes? The participants offered a variety of answers, including one that surprised researchers—the ability to blow out clouds of vapor and do tricks.

Teens have undoubtedly become more interested in vaping tricks due to thousands of online videos demonstrating how to perform them. "Social media plays a big part in this," says James Alexander from National Screening Centers. "Kids use their Instagram, YouTube and Snap Chat accounts to show off their latest smoke tricks. These tricks can be blowing smoke into a circle, blowing huge smoke clouds or exhaling through their nose." Also influential is the growing popularity of "cloud competitions." At these events, vapers compete for cash prizes by blowing the biggest, densest vapor clouds and performing fancy vapor tricks. Even if teens do not attend such competitions, they likely know about them from the Internet.

James Alexander, "The Rise of Vaping Amongst Teens," National Screening Centers, November 8, 2015. www.nationalscreeningcenters.com.

e-cigarettes, compared with fewer than 4 percent of teens who had never vaped.

Friends' viewpoints were found to be of utmost importance in determining whether teens used e-cigarettes. Of those who currently vape, 91 percent said their best friends would react positively to it. This was in stark contrast to the 31 percent of non-vaping teens who said their friends would not react positively to vaping. Boston University School of Public Health professor Michael Siegel says the study's most important implication is that vaping is strongly influenced by peer pressure and peer norms. "That suggests," he says, "that interventions which de-glamorize vaping may be effective in reducing e-cigarette experimentation among youth, just as interventions that de-glamorized smoking helped to greatly reduce smoking rates among young people."[54]

# Brain Development in Progress

Young people may not acknowledge it in surveys, but an important reason why teens are willing to experiment with new activities like vaping is because of their age. Many adolescents are prone to risk-taking behavior, and to some extent this can be attributed to their undeveloped brains—unlike those of adults, adolescents' brains are still in the process of developing. Although it is a fairly recent discovery, scientists now know that the brain is not fully developed until people are in their mid-twenties. "These brain differences don't mean that young people can't make good decisions or tell the difference between right and wrong," says the American Academy of Child & Adolescent Psychiatry. "It also doesn't mean that they shouldn't be held responsible for their actions. But an awareness of these differences can help parents, teachers, advocates, and policy makers understand, anticipate, and manage the behavior of adolescents."[55]

Decades of brain research have shown that the human brain develops from back to front. The prefrontal cortex, which is located directly behind the forehead, is the last part to finish developing. It controls functions such as reasoning, problem solving, impulse control, and decision making. "Adolescents are prone to risky behaviors and impulsive actions that provide instant gratification instead of eventual rewards," says NIDA director Nora D. Volkow. "In part, this is because their prefrontal cortex is still a work in progress." Research has shown that the underdeveloped brain is a major factor in why young people sometimes make poor decisions, such as smoking, taking drugs, or drinking alcohol. "There are numerous pressures in their lives to try these substances (stress and peers, for example)," says Volkow, "but inadequate cognitive resources to help them resist."[56]

Possible impairment to the underdeveloped brain is one of the most serious concerns about youth vaping. This fear is rooted in research showing that when young people smoke, it can cause cognitive damage that may last a lifetime. "Smoking cigarettes during adolescence has been associated with lasting cognitive impairments," says CDC director Thomas R. Frieden, "including memory and attention."[57] Frieden adds that research strongly suggests a connection between nicotine exposure among youth and both long-term structural and functional changes to many different parts of the brain. Although the research he cites was based on nicotine from smoking tobacco cigarettes, nicotine is delivered in aerosol form in most e-cigarettes. Thus, Frieden maintains that vaping poses as much a threat to adolescents as smoking. "Nicotine is dangerous for kids at any age, whether it's an e-cigarette, hookah, cigarette, or a cigar," he says. Frieden's fear is that as e-cigarette prevalence continues to grow among young people, nicotine addiction will grow at the same pace. "We know that nicotine is harmful to the developing brain," he says, "and we could be seeing another generation getting hooked."[58]

> "Nicotine is dangerous for kids at any age, whether it's an e-cigarette, hookah, cigarette, or a cigar."[58]
>
> —Thomas R. Frieden, director of the CDC.

The fear of more teens becoming addicted to nicotine is shared by health officials as well as health care providers. Nicotine is highly addictive, and young people are even more susceptible to addiction than adults. "Nicotine's addictive properties are a risk for any age group, but with adolescents, the stakes are even higher," says K. Vendrell Rankin, director of Texas A&M University Baylor College of Dentistry's Tobacco Treatment Services. The younger users are when they first try nicotine, the more likely they are to struggle with nicotine addiction throughout their lives. This is because nicotine receptors begin to develop as soon as the brain is exposed to nicotine, as Rankin explains: "Everybody has a certain amount of nicotine receptors in the brain. When you start smoking, vaping or supplying nicotine to them, they multiply. If you stop smoking or vaping, the receptors don't go away."[59]

# A Gateway to Smoking?

As vaping's popularity continues to grow among teens, health officials and health care providers fear that teen smoking rates will also rise. For years they have breathed a collective sigh of relief as teen smoking rates have continued to steadily decline. Back in 1997 the MTF survey showed that 28 percent of American high school students smoked, but by 2015 the rate had plummeted to 7 percent. For anyone in the field of health care, that is cause for celebration—but with the fast-growing popularity of vaping among teens, the fear is that smoking could once again be considered acceptable or be "renormalized." Stanford University School of Medicine physician Robert Jackler is one health care professional who is troubled by the possibility that e-cigarettes could renormalize tobacco and smoking among youth. "If you look at the way it is with an e-cigarette, it absolutely replicates the hand-to-mouth ritual of smoking," says Jackler. "It satisfies that primordial urge to suck on something, so a person who's vaping looks like someone who's smoking."[60]

Exploring the possible connection between vaping and the onset of tobacco smoking has been a high priority for researchers such as Lauren Dutra of the University of California–San Francisco's Center for Tobacco Control Research and Education. In 2014 Dutra led a study of middle and high school students. She and her colleagues found that teens who used e-cigarettes were more likely to smoke tobacco cigarettes and less likely to quit smoking once they started. In addition, the study revealed that vaping was associated with higher odds of teens progressing from experimenting with cigarettes to becoming established smokers. "Despite claims that e-cigarettes are helping quit smoking," says Dutra, "we found that e-cigarettes were associated with more, not less, cigarette smoking among adolescents." She adds, "E-cigarettes are likely to be gateway devices for nicotine addiction among youth, opening up a whole new market for tobacco."[61]

Hawaii is one state in which health officials are extremely concerned about teen e-cigarette use being a gateway to smoking. Surveys have found that between 25 percent and 30 percent of ninth- and tenth-grade students have vaped at least once, and about 18 percent use e-cigarettes regularly. To determine whether e-cigarette use among adolescents leads to tobacco smoking, researchers from the University of Hawaii surveyed more than two thousand ninth and tenth graders from high schools on the island of Oahu. The surveys were conducted in 2013 and again in 2014. Researchers found that teens who had used e-cigarettes were

# Teens Favor E-Cigarettes
# Over Traditional Cigarettes

According to CDC research, e-cigarette use among teens has increased, while use of traditional cigarettes, cigars, and smokeless tobacco has decreased. Although health officials are encouraged by the decline in popularity of traditional tobacco products among teens, they are concerned about the rising use of e-cigarettes. One reason is that e-cigarettes usually contain nicotine. Health officials say that nicotine is dangerous for young people because it can cause lasting cognitive impairment in their still-developing brains.

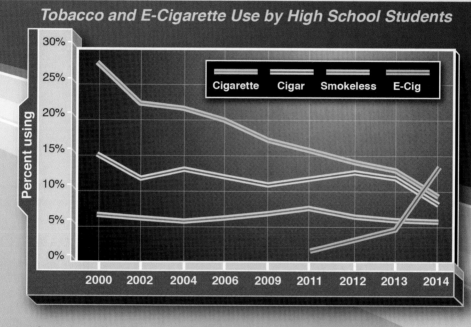

*Tobacco and E-Cigarette Use by High School Students*

Source: Jesse Rifkin, "E-Cigarettes Are Now More Popular Among Young People than Regular Cigarettes," *Huffington Post*, April 16, 2015. www.huffingtonpost.com.

far more likely than their nonvaping peers to try regular cigarettes sometime during the following year. In their January 2016 report, the study authors state, "We found that e-cigarettes had a risk-promoting effect for the onset of smoking."[62]

The authors acknowledge that exactly why e-cigarettes serve as a gateway to smoking is unknown. They offer some theories, however, such as the fact that e-cigarettes mimic the look and feel of cigarettes. Also, they write, "the inhaling and

*Some researchers theorize that inhaling and exhaling e-cigarette vapor and smoking regular cigarettes produce the same sensory experiences. This, they say, is one reason that vaping leads teens to try cigarette smoking.*

exhaling of e-cigarette aerosol produces some of the same sensory experiences as smoking a cigarette." The authors suggest that this similarity may contribute to the inclination to try tobacco cigarettes. Also, once teens experience the effects of nicotine via vaping, they may be tempted to try tobacco cigarettes "in order to get a bigger 'kick.'" Overall, they emphasize that this study, together with other findings about adolescents, vaping, and smoking, suggest that "policies restricting adolescents' access to e-cigarettes may have a rationale from a public health standpoint."[63]

## Vaping to Get High

As the incidence of vaping has grown among teens, a new trend has emerged: using vape pens to smoke marijuana. High schools throughout the United States have reported an increase in pot vaping among young people. One example is a high school in Lakewood, Colorado, where in 2014 school officials became aware that teens were vaping pot—and they were doing it during class. "Teachers are aware of what to look for," says principal Ron Castagna. "The nervous habit of biting on your pen has a new meaning to it."[64]

In 2014 researchers from Oberlin College and Yale University conducted the first study to examine pot vaping prevalence among teens. More than thirty-eight hundred high school students in southeastern Connecticut took part in the study. They filled out anonymous surveys with questions like "Which of the following have you used to smoke marijuana?" Several of the listed choices related to vaping, such as e-cigarettes filled with hash oil and portable vaporizers filled with dried marijuana.

The study revealed that vaporizing cannabis was common among three groups: teens who had used e-cigarettes (of these, 18 percent had vaped cannabis); teens who had smoked marijuana (of these, 18.4 percent had vaped cannabis); and teens who had done both (of these, 26.5 percent had vaped cannabis). Study coauthor Meghan E. Morean says that vape pens give kids a way to hide what they are inhaling. "It's so much easier to conceal e-cigarette pot use. Everybody knows that characteristic smell of marijuana, but this vapor is different. It's possible that teenagers are using pot in a much less detectable way."[65]

Health officials are alarmed about the growing popularity of pot vaping among teens for a number of reasons, one of which is potential damage to their underdeveloped brains. Scientists cannot say for certain that marijuana will harm young people's brains, but they are very concerned about the possibility. Another concern is that many teens are vaping highly concentrated hash oil or waxes infused with tetrahydrocannabinol (THC), the psychoactive ingredient in cannabis. The potency of these substances exceeds that of dried cannabis by as much as thirty times. "It's a lot stronger high when you smoke it through the e-cigs,"[66] says Hayley Franklin, director of an antidrug

> "It's so much easier to conceal e-cigarette pot use. Everybody knows that characteristic smell of marijuana, but this vapor is different."[65]
>
> —Meghan E. Morean, a researcher at Oberlin College in Oberlin, Ohio.

organization in Carroll County, Kentucky. Scientists warn that the higher the levels of THC, the higher the risk for lasting changes to the adolescent brain.

## Growing Concerns

Health officials have many worries about the growing prevalence of e-cigarettes and vaping, but by far they are most concerned about young people. Surveys have shown that at the same time vaping's popularity is soaring, teens have little or no awareness that the practice can be potentially harmful. Because their brains are still developing, inhaling nicotine could cause cognitive im-

# Vaping Synthetic Drugs

As the popularity of teen vaping has escalated, health officials have become aware of a disturbing new trend: vaping synthetic drugs. These drugs include Spice or K2 (called synthetic marijuana), flakka, N-Bomb, and synthetic cathinones (bath salts). Potent, powerful, and unpredictable, they are usually imported from other countries, and people who use them have no way of knowing where they came from, who made them, or exactly what is in them. One of these, a liquid called Cloud Nine, is part of the bath salts family—and these have nothing to do with bathing. These drugs have effects similar to methamphetamine but may be up to ten times more powerful, and health officials say they are some of the most dangerous drugs that exist.

Although it is unknown exactly how many teens are vaping drugs like Cloud Nine, there has been a spike throughout the country in emergency room visits related to their use. In 2014, for example, four high school students from Canton, Michigan, were hospitalized after using Cloud Nine, and three of them had vaped the drug. Canton Township deputy police chief Debra Newsome describes the students' physical effects from vaping the drug: "Hallucinations, nausea, vomiting, extreme high heart rate which is causing medical experts a great amount of concern."

Quoted in Roger Weber, "Plymouth-Canton Students Hospitalized on 'Cloud Nine' Drug," Click on Detroit, September 12, 2014. www.clickondetroit.com.

pairments and/or hook them into being addicted—which, some studies suggest, could potentially lead to tobacco smoking. Also, the emerging trend of vaping marijuana is posing a whole new set of concerns about the effects of vaping on youth. These are challenging issues that need to be addressed in the coming years, and health officials consider this among their highest priorities.

Some young people also see the urgency of addressing the youth vaping craze, including Kaylee Musick, a teen from Virginia. "Vaping is the cool thing to do right now, so a lot of kids are trying it just to say they have," she says. An avid runner, Musick has not tried e-cigarettes and has no intention of doing so. "I don't see it being safe, no matter what they try to tell you," she says. "They used to say cigarettes were safe, too, right?" Musick grew up in a family of smokers, and she fears that vaping among teens could lead to smoking. "Not all my friends think like that, though," she says. "If kids think it is safe and cool, they might just try it—and that is what people should be worried about."[67]

> "I don't see [vaping] being safe, no matter what they try to tell you. They used to say cigarettes were safe, too, right?"[67]
>
> —Kaylee Musick, a teen from Virginia.

# CHAPTER 5: How Should E-Cigarettes Be Regulated?

In May 2015 the alternative newspaper *Philadelphia Weekly* ran a four-page color ad about the city's upcoming Smokin' Summer concert series. The ad was paid for by Lorillard, the tobacco company that owns blu e-cigarettes, and it was reminiscent of cigarette advertising from decades ago. "Cigarette brands are no longer allowed to sponsor sports and entertainment events," says the Campaign for Tobacco-Free Kids, "but e-cigarette brands still do."[68] That statement refers to the lack of federal control over e-cigarette advertising. By law Lorillard and other companies can no longer advertise tobacco products in print or on radio or television, but there is no such law governing e-cigarettes. As a result, e-cigarette advertising is widespread—and is often designed to appeal to youth.

One example is a series of ads for blu that features popular actor Stephen Dorff. The ads appear in a number of magazines, including *Cosmopolitan* and *Sports Illustrated*, which both have high teen readership. "These ads echo the tobacco industry's long history of using celebrities to market their products," says the Campaign for Tobacco-Free Kids. The group adds that with such youth-oriented marketing, it is no wonder teen e-cigarette use is on the rise. "The Food and Drug Administration must quickly finalize its proposed rule to regulate all tobacco products, including e-cigarettes, and stop the marketing and sale of these products to kids," says the group. "Without FDA oversight, the irresponsible marketing of e-cigarettes threatens our nation's kids and health."[69]

## Like the "Wild West"

E-cigarette advertising is legal because it is not subject to FDA regulation. Unlike tobacco cigarettes, e-cigarettes (unless marketed for therapeutic purposes) do not fall under the auspices of the FDA. The extraordinarily fast rise in vaping's popularity and booming e-cigarette sales have led to widespread alarm over the lack of federal regulatory oversight. One concerned physician is Brett Belchetz, who practices emergency medicine in Toronto, Canada, where regulatory oversight of e-cigarettes is also lacking. He says:

> This drastic growth rate has left governments scrambling to create new legislation to regulate these products. With no existing laws addressing where e-cigarettes can be consumed, or where and to whom they can be sold, the current situation has been described as akin to a "Wild West" by prominent figures in health and education, where anyone—even minors—can purchase e-cigarettes and use them in nearly any setting.[70]

In the United States the FDA is working diligently to change that scenario. As part of the US Department of Health and Human Services, the FDA is charged with protecting public health. The agency is accountable for ensuring the safety and effectiveness of food, medicines, drugs, medical devices, and a host of other products. Since June 2009, when the Obama administration enacted the Family Smoking Prevention and Tobacco Control Act, the FDA has also been in control of the tobacco industry. This includes overseeing the manufacturing, marketing, and distribution of tobacco products to protect public health and reduce tobacco use by minors.

Although the Tobacco Control Act does not allow the FDA to regulate e-cigarettes, it contains a process called the "deeming rule" for the agency to use to gain oversight responsibility. A July 2014 article in the journal *Health Affairs* explains: "The law does give the FDA

> "With no existing laws addressing where e-cigarettes can be consumed, or where and to whom they can be sold, the current situation has been described as akin to a 'Wild West.'"[70]
>
> —Brett Belchetz, an emergency medicine physician from Toronto, Canada.

# More Advertising Equals More Youth Vaping

When the FDA released its final e-cigarette regulations in 2015, the proposal contained nothing about advertising. Rather, the new rules focused mainly on banning sales of e-cigarettes and vaping supplies to minors and tougher restrictions for manufacturers and sellers. Officials from the CDC and other health-related agencies were dismayed by the absence of advertising regulations. Studies have clearly shown that the steady rise in e-cigarette use among youth has matched growth in dollars spent on advertising for these products.

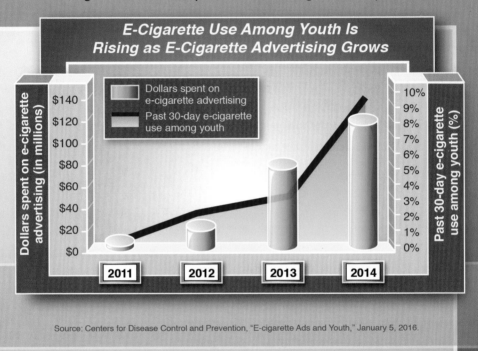

**E-Cigarette Use Among Youth Is Rising as E-Cigarette Advertising Grows**

Source: Centers for Disease Control and Prevention, "E-cigarette Ads and Youth," January 5, 2016.

authority to 'deem' other products that meet the statutory defini-
tion of tobacco—a product 'made or derived from tobacco' and
'intended for human consumption'—as subject to its regulatory
oversight."[71] Because nicotine is derived from tobacco, and most
e-cigarettes and e-liquid contain nicotine, these products would
eventually be subject to FDA regulation under the Tobacco Control Act. This is, however, a long, complex, multiple-step process
with no guaranteed completion date.

In October 2015 the FDA finalized its recommendations for
regulating e-cigarettes. If these are eventually put into law, e-

cigarettes will be regulated by the agency in the same way that tobacco cigarettes are today. Among other changes, the new law would ban e-cigarette sales to anyone under age eighteen and require health warning labels on e-cigarettes stating that they contain nicotine, an addictive drug. Free samples of e-cigarettes will be banned, as will vending machine sales of e-cigarettes except in places where minors are not allowed. In addition, to ensure consistency and safety, e-cigarette manufacturers will be required to register their products and report their ingredients to the FDA. The products will also be subject to periodic FDA inspections. "You won't be able to mix nicotine in your bathtub and sell it anymore,"[72] says David B. Abrams, executive director of the antismoking research group Schroeder Institute for Tobacco Research and Policy Studies.

## Not Tough Enough?

Health officials and e-cigarette opponents say these restrictions are important first steps but stop far short of what is needed. For instance, the new law does not ban minors from purchasing e-cigarettes online, which research has shown is common and surprisingly easy. Even though websites that sell vaping supplies technically require buyers to be eighteen or older, there is rarely any verification to ensure that they are. New York physician David Samadi has tested this himself and says online accessibility is a big problem. He writes, "E-cigarette companies . . . promise sophisticated age-verification technology to limit access to minors. Well, I visited one company, BluCigs.com, to see for myself. What I found was a very simple popup, and with one click, I was in. I have a hard time believing this would slow down our tech-savvy teens."[73]

> "You won't be able to mix nicotine in your bathtub and sell it anymore."[72]
>
> —David B. Abrams, executive director of the antismoking research group Schroeder Institute for Tobacco Research and Policy Studies.

One aspect of the proposed FDA e-cigarette regulation that is highly controversial relates to flavors—the FDA will not place any restrictions on the types and varieties of flavors that manufacturers offer. Health officials and youth advocacy groups are convinced that manufacturers deliberately target young people with many of the flavors they offer. The manufacturers deny those claims, arguing that adults like fun flavors too. But according to a 2014 report by the Campaign for Tobacco-Free Kids, it is obvious that youth are being targeted. The report cites nine e-juice flavors that the group calls "some of the most egregious, youth-oriented e-cigarette flavors we've found."[74] The flavors are banana split, cotton candy, Kool-Aid, Sweet Tarts, Hawaiian Punch, Rocket Pop, Gummy Bears, Froot Loops, and Skittles.

Another point of contention about the FDA's proposed e-cigarette regulation is that it will not restrict marketing. This includes everything from in-store displays and TV advertising to billboards and magazine ads. Stanford School of Medicine physician Robert Jackler compares today's e-cigarette marketing with the cigarette advertising that has been outlawed for decades. "All those styles of advertising have come back in the absolutely unregulated environment of e-cigarettes," says Jackler. "So you have television, including the Superbowl, and radio ads. You have pictures of doctors enjoying e-cigarettes, connoting their healthfulness."[75]

Jackler is one of numerous health care professionals who strongly favor federal restrictions on e-cigarette advertising. In a January 2016 poll of more than twenty-five hundred physicians, 90 percent said that e-cigarette advertising should be regulated similarly to tobacco cigarette advertising. "Teens are being inundated with advertisements for e-cigarettes that make smoking look cool and sexy," says New Jersey physician Linda Girgis. "They are being encouraged by the tobacco companies to take up this nasty habit that could have deadly consequences. We need to limit teens' exposure to these e-cigarette advertisements to keep them from getting hooked."[76]

## Unsettled Science

The FDA is aware that its impending regulation is not as restrictive as it needs to be. FDA officials acknowledge the increase in e-cigarette use by young people, the availability of fruit- and

# Legislating Online Vaping Sales

North Carolina is among the states that have implemented laws to prevent young people from buying e-cigarettes and other vaping supplies. Age verification is required to purchase vapor products, and it is a Class II misdemeanor to sell or distribute them to anyone under age eighteen. Yet according to a study released in March 2015, North Carolina teens who want to vape easily get around these laws by buying e-cigarettes online.

Over a period of four months, eleven nonsmoking teens aged fourteen to seventeen shopped for e-cigarettes from ninety-eight of the most popular online vendors. When other factors were accounted for, they were successful 93.7 percent of the time. The packages were delivered to the teens' homes, and the shipping companies made no attempts to verify their ages. In fact, nearly all packages were simply left at the door. The study authors write: "In the absence of federal regulations, youth e-cigarette use has increased and e-cigarette sellers online operate in a regulatory vacuum, using few, if any, efforts to prevent sales to minors."

Rebecca S. Williams, Jason Demick, and Kurt M. Ribisl, "Electronic Cigarette Sales to Minors via the Internet," *JAMA Pediatrics*, March 2015. www.researchgate.net.

candy-flavored e-cigarette liquid, and the problem of unregulated marketing. But the agency maintains that further restrictions cannot be enacted until there is scientific proof that e-cigarettes are harmful. "We do not currently have sufficient data about these products to determine what effects e-cigarettes have on the public health,"[77] says the FDA.

Numerous studies are underway, but no one can say when the science surrounding e-cigarettes and vaping will be settled. So even though many well-intentioned people, including some health officials, are urging the FDA to hurry the process along, the agency believes it is prudent to proceed cautiously. In a June 2014 editorial, RAND Corporation senior behavioral scientists William G. Shadel, Joan Tucker, and Steven Martino express their support for the agency's careful, measured approach. "At this point," they write, "asking the FDA to restrict marketing and advertising or to ban flavored products would be premature. The base of

*An advertisement touts the so-called advantages of e-cigarettes over traditional ones. E-cigarette marketing is unrestricted, which youth advocates say enables manufacturers to deliberately target young people.*

scientific evidence grows with each new study, particularly with e-cigarettes, but it doesn't support additional regulatory action beyond what the FDA has already proposed—at least not yet."[78]

## State Action

In the absence of federal regulatory oversight, most states have enacted their own legislation. Only ten states still allow minors to buy e-cigarettes, e-liquid, and other vaping paraphernalia. These are Maine, Massachusetts, Michigan, Montana, Nevada, New Mexico, North Dakota, Oregon, Pennsylvania, and Texas. The remaining forty states have laws that ban the sale of e-cigarettes to minors, but other components of the legislation differ widely from state to state. Minnesota and North Carolina, for instance, are the only states that tax e-cigarettes, and some others restrict where vaping is permissible. In five states, the legislation forbids municipalities from passing stricter vaping ordinances than what the state laws cover.

For the most part, states did not pass these laws to restrict the overall sale and use of e-cigarettes. Rather, their intent was to keep young people from buying the devices. "My No. 1 concern was to make them illegal for purchase by kids as fast as we could," says Ohio state representative Stephanie Kunze. "These things look like Sephora eyeliner and they taste like Dr. Pepper."[79]

# The Public Weighs In

As with other aspects of the e-cigarette debate (and smoking in general), most people have strong opinions about e-cigarette regulation. When asked their opinions about the issue, the majority have expressed that they are in favor of regulation. For example, during an August 2015 survey conducted by National Public Radio, nearly 60 percent of participants believed e-cigarettes should be regulated by the FDA as tobacco products are. Interestingly, one factor that has been revealed in surveys is the public's lack of awareness that the devices are not already regulated. Most said they had no idea that e-cigarettes were not subject to the same or similar restrictions as tobacco cigarettes.

Adults are not the only ones who have strong opinions about e-cigarette regulation; young people are also willing to speak their minds on the topic. This was revealed during a September 2015 survey that involved more than fifteen hundred parents and six hundred teens. More than half of the parents (54 percent) and 62 percent of the teens said that it is currently easy for people under age eighteen to buy e-cigarettes. Nearly all parents (93 percent) and almost as many teens (87 percent) said they support laws that restrict sales of e-cigarettes to minors. A large majority of parents (84 percent) and teens (81 percent) believe that allowing minors to use e-cigarettes will encourage the use of other tobacco products. When asked about the banning of candy- and fruit-flavored e-cigarettes and e-liquid, 64 percent of parents and 71 percent of teens said yes, the products should be banned. The news release states: "The high degree of agreement between parents of teens and the teens themselves regarding e-cigarettes may indicate deeply shared mutual concern about tobacco-containing products as clear health hazards."[80]

# A Contentious Debate

Since the FDA first publicized its intention to regulate e-cigarettes, the issue has been embroiled in controversy. According to vaping advocates, regulating e-cigarettes as tobacco products is overkill and even constitutes government overreach. The devices do not burn tobacco like cigarettes. In fact, their only connection to tobacco is the nicotine content. As American Vaping Association president Gregory Conley has stated, "E-cigarettes are not tobacco products and should not be regulated as such."[81]

The most impassioned objections to the FDA's proposed regulations are economic in nature—that regulation could drive small e-cigarette and e-liquid manufacturers out of business. According to Conley, as many as 99 percent of small businesses in the vaping industry could be forced to close as a result of FDA actions. This fear is shared by Sean Gore, chair of the Oklahoma Vapor Advocacy League. Gore says that small vaping businesses, which make up a large percentage of the e-cigarette market,

Kim Thompson stands outside her vaping shop in Lakewood, Washington. Vaping advocates say that proposed FDA regulation of e-cigarettes will drive small vaping stores like Thompson's out of business.

will not be able to afford the costs of testing that the FDA will require, as well as other costs that will likely be associated with more stringent regulation. Big tobacco companies, however, could easily afford these high costs, which leads some people to conclude that the FDA's regulations are largely economic in nature. "We're just going to hand the industry straight back to them, while driving small business owners out?," Gore asks. "It makes no sense." The challenges associated with regulation would be especially insurmountable for small e-cigarette businesses if the FDA requires that every new flavor be tested for safety. "If that happens, you will end up seeing probably five flavors,"[82] says Gore.

> **"E-cigarettes are not tobacco products and should not be regulated as such."[81]**
>
> —Gregory Conley, president of the American Vaping Association.

Ryan Bixby feels exactly the same way. He manages a vaping shop in Washington, DC, called DC Vape Joint. He says that in order to comply with regulation of e-liquid flavors, companies would have to spend $250,000 per flavor, per nicotine strength. "The rules are completely designed to push the small companies out of the market,"[83] says Bixby.

Those whose main concern is public health argue that tough regulation of e-cigarettes is absolutely necessary. As much as they do not want to force any businesses to close, they are adamant that people who make and sell e-cigarettes and e-liquid must be required to comply with safety standards. This is the perspective of Matthew Myers, president of the Campaign for Tobacco-Free Kids. He opines:

> The notion that people who have no chemical training, no safety training are mixing concoctions in the back room or their bathtub and giving it to the consumer means we're doing a human guinea pig experiment on literally millions of Americans without any knowledge of what the consequences are. If you're too small a manufacturer in order to be able to assure the public about what's in your product, then you shouldn't be selling it to the public.[84]

## An Unforeseen, Unfortunate Consequence

As the debate over e-cigarette regulation continues, a possible offshoot of tough new rules is one that health officials consider unacceptable: that the years-long declining rate of tobacco smokers would start to swing upward again. According to Boston University School of Public Health professor Michael Siegel, the growing prevalence of vaping has helped with smoking's decline.

"E-cigarettes are denormalizing smoking,"[85] he says. Siegel adds, though, that if FDA restrictions make e-cigarettes too difficult for people to buy, those who have been vaping instead of

## Why Risk It?

Illinois is one of the states with e-cigarette legislation in place. Like those in most other states, the Illinois law was primarily designed to keep youth from buying the devices, but Chicago legislators wanted to do more to protect teens from the potential harms of vaping. So in December 2015, Chicago mayor Rahm Emanuel and the Department of Public Health launched an educational campaign called Vaping: Why Risk It? The campaign aims to raise awareness among youth of the dangers of vaping by emphasizing three areas of concern: the highly addictive nature of nicotine; the toxic chemicals that can be contained in e-liquids; and the lack of regulation, which means no one knows how manufacturers make the vaping products or exactly what they contain.

The Why Risk It? campaign features a series of digital and outdoor advertisements, tool kits for community and tobacco-prevention organizations, and a compelling presence on social media. "E-cigarettes and other electronic nicotine devices are designed to act like cigarettes," says public health commissioner Julie Morita, "with flavors that appeal to children. Chicagoans must know the real health risks associated with using these products. This new campaign will help keep our young people from ever trying these dangerous, addictive products."

Quoted in City of Chicago, "Mayor Emanuel and the Department of Public Health Announce Campaign to Reduce and Prevent Youth Vaping," press release, December 23, 2015. www.cityofchicago.org.

smoking may return to smoking. He cites a national survey released in January 2016, in which thousands of respondents said they would still be smoking if e-cigarettes had not become available.

The survey was conducted in November and December 2015 and involved more than 20,000 vapers. Of those, 17,176 said that using e-cigarettes had helped them quit smoking. Nearly all of these former smokers reported that they would still be smoking were it not for e-cigarettes. When asked if the FDA's e-cigarette regulation were adopted in its present form, 21 percent of former smokers said they would return to smoking. In addition, 46 percent of dual users (cigarettes and e-cigarettes) said they would increase the amount that they smoke. "This," says Siegel, "is what I might call the renormalization of smoking."[86]

## The Controversy Continues

Strict regulation of e-cigarettes has both supporters and opponents, and each side is equally passionate about its views. People who advocate tough FDA restrictions argue that currently, consumers have no way of knowing what is contained in e-cigarettes or e-liquid, and their health and safety are at stake. Supporters of regulation are especially concerned about young people because the popularity of e-cigarettes among teens has soared in recent years. Most who argue against tough regulation agree that young people need to be protected. Their argument is that tough restrictions are uncalled for as well as premature, since the science of vaping is not yet settled. As scientists continue to study the health effects of vaping and gain a more in-depth understanding of e-cigarettes, the regulation controversy may eventually be resolved. According to some industry experts, however, that may be years in the making.

# SOURCE NOTES

## Chapter 1: A Growing Trend

1. Quoted in Barbara Demick, "A High-Tech Approach to Getting a Nicotine Fix," *Los Angeles Times*, April 25, 2009. http://articles.latimes.com.
2. Keith Wagstaff, "Vaping 101: How Do E-Cigarettes Work?," NBC News, April 24, 2014. www.nbcnews.com.
3. Britt E. Erickson, "Boom in E-Cigarettes Sparks Call for Regulation," *Chemical & Engineering News*, February 16, 2015. http://cen.acs.org.
4. Quoted in Simon Akam, "Big Tobacco Fights Back: How the Cigarette Kings Bought the Vaping Industry," *Newsweek*, May 27, 2015. http://europe.newsweek.com.
5. World Lung Foundation, "E-Cigarettes," *Tobacco Atlas*, 2015. www.tobaccoatlas.org.
6. National Institute on Drug Abuse, "Electronic Cigarettes (E-Cigarettes)," August 2015. www.drugabuse.gov.
7. Quoted in Fines Massey, "E-Cigarettes Appeal to Ex-smokers, Hobbyists," *Lebanon (MO) Daily Record*, November 13, 2015. www.lebanondailyrecord.com.
8. Quoted in KU Leuven "E-Cigarettes Significantly Reduce Tobacco Cravings," news release, November 19, 2014. www.kuleuven.be.
9. Quoted in R. Morgan Griffin, "E-Cigarettes 101," WebMD, November 18, 2015. www.webmd.com.
10. Robert Jackler, "5 Questions: Jackler on the Rise of E-Cigarettes," Stanford Medicine News Center, March 5, 2014. https://med.stanford.edu.
11. Quoted in Sabrina Tavernise, "Use of E-Cigarettes Rises Sharply Among Teenagers, Report Says," *New York Times*, April 16, 2015. www.nytimes.com.
12. Quoted in Kimberly Leonard, "E-Cigarette Use Triples Among Teens," *U.S. News & World Report*, April 16, 2015. www.usnews.com.

13. Quoted in Tavernise, "Use of E-Cigarettes Rises Sharply Among Teenagers, Report Says."

14. Quoted in Jilian Mincer, "As Youth Vaping Rises, Teens Cite the Allure of Tricks," *Reuters*, May 1, 2015. www.reuters.com.

15. Quoted in T.R. Goldman, "E-Cigarettes and Federal Regulation (Updated)," *Health Affairs*, July 18, 2014. www.health affairs.org.

## Chapter 2: What Are the Effects of E-Cigarettes?

16. Aruni Bhatnagar et al., "AHA Policy Statement: Electronic Cigarettes," *Circulation*, August 24, 2014. http://circ.ahajour nals.org.

17. Quoted in David Nather and Sheila Kaplan, "E-Cigarettes Widely Seen as Harmful in STAT-Harvard Poll," STAT, November 9, 2015. www.statnews.com.

18. Jason (Mike Floorwalker), "10 Facts That Everyone Gets Wrong About Vaping," *Gizmodo* (blog), November 19, 2014. http://gizmodo.com.

19. Jacob Grier, "The War on 'Vaping' Is Misguided: Guest Opinion," *Oregonian* (Portland, OR), March 8, 2014. www.oregon live.com.

20. Brett Belchetz, "Health Risks of Vaping Still Unknown: Doctor," *Toronto Sun*, July 4, 2015. www.torontosun.com.

21. Avrum Spira, interviewed by Sara Rimer, "Behind the Vapor," *BU Today* (Boston University), October 20, 2014. www .bu.edu.

22. Spira, interviewed by Rimer, "Behind the Vapor."

23. Quoted in Madison Park, "Your Body Immediately After Vaping an E-Cigarette," Yahoo!, August 28, 2015. www.yahoo .com.

24. Spira, interviewed by Rimer, "Behind the Vapor."

25. Quoted in Rob Stein, "E-Cigarettes Can Churn Out High Levels of Formaldehyde," NPR, January 22, 2015. www.npr.org.

26. Quoted in Stein, "E-Cigarettes Can Churn Out High Levels of Formaldehyde."

27. Spira, interviewed by Rimer, "Behind the Vapor."

28. Spira, interviewed by Rimer, "Behind the Vapor."

29. Quoted in Amy Roeder, "Chemical Flavorings Found in E-Cigarettes Linked to Lung Disease," *Harvard Gazette*, December 8, 2015. http://news.harvard.edu.

30. Raquel Rutledge, "Lab Tests Reveal Popular E-Cigarette Liquids Contain Harmful Chemicals," *Milwaukee Journal Sentinel*, October 20, 2015. www.jsonline.com.

31. Quoted in Meredith Kile, "7 Things You Need to Know About Electronic Cigarettes," Al Jazeera America, November 5, 2013. http://america.aljazeera.com.

32. Quoted in Matt Richtel, "Selling a Poison by the Barrel: Liquid Nicotine for E-Cigarettes," *New York Times*, March 23, 2014. www.nytimes.com.

## Chapter 3: Are E-Cigarettes Addictive?

33. Frank Bures, "Dr. Frank Bures: Nicotine Addiction Is Powerful, Dangerous," *Winona (MN) Daily News*, September 21, 2014. www.winonadailynews.com.

34. Roy A. Beveridge, "E-Cigarettes: Let's Not Make the Same Mistake Twice," *Forbes*, May 23, 2014. www.forbes.com.

35. Quoted in Nather and Kaplan, "E-Cigarettes Widely Seen as Harmful in STAT-Harvard Poll."

36. Rachael Lloyd, "I Thought My E-Cigarette Was a Miracle. Turns Out, I Was Smoking the Equivalent of 40-a-Day," *Telegraph* (London), August 27, 2014. www.telegraph.co.uk.

37. Nick Green, "Don't Believe the Hype: E-Cigarettes Won't Ruin Society, They Changed My Life," *Guardian* (Manchester), December 18, 2013. www.theguardian.com.

38. Nora D. Volkow, preface to *Drugs, Brains, and Behavior: The Science of Addiction*, by National Institute on Drug Abuse, July 2014. https://teens.drugabuse.gov.

39. National Institute on Drug Abuse, *Drugs, Brains, and Behavior: The Science of Addiction*.

40. National Institute on Drug Abuse, "Nicotine," June 2007. www.drugabuse.gov.

41. National Institute on Drug Abuse, "Nicotine."

42. Matt McConnell, "How Much Nicotine Is in One Cigarette?," Electronic Cigarette Consumer Reviews, March 18, 2015. www.electroniccigaretteconsumerreviews.com.

43. Quoted in Jilian Mincer, "E-Cigarette Usage Surges in Past Year: Reuters/Ipsos Poll," *Reuters*, June 10, 2015. www.reuters.com.

44. Quoted in Jennifer Abbasi, "E-Cigarettes Less Addictive than Cigarettes," Pennsylvania State University, December 9, 2014. http://news.psu.edu.

45. Quoted in Ashley Welch, "E-Cigarettes May Be Just as Addictive as the Real Thing," CBS News, July 24, 2015. www.cbsnews.com.

46. Ahmad El-Hellani et al., "Free-Base and Protonated Nicotine in Electronic Cigarette Liquids and Aerosols," *Chemical Research in Toxicology*, July 9, 2015. www.researchgate.net.

47. Hillel R. Alpert, Israel T. Agaku, and Gregory N. Connolly, "A Study of Pyrazines in Cigarettes and How Additives Might Be Used to Enhance Tobacco Addiction," *Tobacco Control*, June 10, 2015. http://m.tobaccocontrol.bmj.com.

48. Mandy Stadtmiller, "How I Finally Quit E-Cigarettes Along with the Rest of Those Super-Addictive Vaping and Nicotine Replacement Products," XOJane, March 24, 2014. www.xojane.com.

49. Stadtmiller, "How I Finally Quit E-Cigarettes Along with the Rest of Those Super-Addictive Vaping and Nicotine Replacement Products."

## Chapter 4: What Risks Do E-Cigarettes Pose to Youth?

50. Quoted in Sasha Keenan et al., "Vape Culture Attracts Teens, Poses Harmful Risks," *Huffington Post*, September 29, 2015. www.huffingtonpost.com.

51. Quoted in Keenan et al., "Vape Culture Attracts Teens, Poses Harmful Risks."

52. Quoted in Jared Wadley and Janice Lee, "Most Youth Use E-Cigarettes for Novelty, Flavors—Not to Quit Smoking," University of Michigan News, December 16, 2015. http://ns.umich.edu.

53. Quoted in Wadley and Lee, "Most Youth Use E-Cigarettes for Novelty, Flavors—Not to Quit Smoking."

54. Quoted in Tara Haelle, "Are E-Cigarettes' Popularity Causing More Teens to Smoke?," *Forbes*, July 27, 2015. www.forbes.com.

55. American Academy of Child & Adolescent Psychiatry, "The Teen Brain: Behavior, Problem Solving, and Decision Making," *Facts for Families*, December 2011. www.aacap.org.

56. Nora D. Volkow, "Brain in Progress: Why Teens Can't Always Resist Temptation," *TEDMED blog*, January 27, 2015. http://blog.tedmed.com.

57. Quoted in Centers for Disease Control and Prevention, "Transcript for CDC Press Briefing: E-Cigarette Use Triples Among Middle and High School Students in Just One Year," April 16, 2015. www.cdc.gov.

58. Quoted in Centers for Disease Control and Prevention, "Transcript for CDC Press Briefing."

59. Quoted in Jennifer Fuentes-Tamu, "Does Vaping Prep Teens for Lifelong Addiction?," *Futurity*, August 25, 2015. www.futurity.org.

60. Jackler, "5 Questions."

61. Quoted in Elizabeth Fernandez, "E-Cigarettes: Gateway to Nicotine Addiction for U.S. Teens, Says UCSF Study," UCSF News Center, March 6, 2014. www.ucsf.edu.

62. Thomas A. Wills et al., "Longitudinal Study of E-Cigarette Use and Onset of Cigarette Smoking Among High School Students in Hawaii," *Tobacco Control*, January 2016. http://tobaccocontrol.bmj.com.

63. Wills et al., "Longitudinal Study of E-Cigarette Use and Onset of Cigarette Smoking Among High School Students in Hawaii."

64. Quoted in Jaimie E. Goldstein, "Students Find Way to Secretly Smoke Marijuana in Class," CBS Denver, February 5, 2014. http://denver.cbslocal.com.

65. Quoted in Christine Rushton, "Teens Find a New Use for E-Cigarettes: Vaping Marijuana," *USA Today*, September 7, 2015. http://denver.cbslocal.com.

66. Quoted in Erica Coghill, "Teenagers Using E-Cigarettes to Get High," WLKY, January 7, 2015. www.wlky.com.

67. Quoted in Richard V. Homan, "Up in Smoke," *EVMS Magazine*, 2016. www.evms.edu.

# Chapter 5: How Should E-Cigarettes Be Regulated?

68. Editor, "E-Cigarette Marketing Continues to Mirror Cigarette Marketing," *Tobacco Unfiltered* (blog), Campaign for Tobacco-Free Kids, June 17, 2015. www.tobaccofreekids.org.
69. Editor, "E-Cigarette Marketing Continues to Mirror Cigarette Marketing."
70. Brett Belchetz, "The Unadvertised Health Risks of E-Cigarettes," *Huffington Post*, March 6, 2015. www.huffingtonpost.ca.
71. T.R. Goldman, "E-Cigarettes and Federal Regulation," *Health Affairs*, July 18, 2014. www.healthaffairs.org.
72. Quoted in Sabrina Tavernise, "F.D.A. Will Propose New Regulations for E-Cigarettes," *New York Times*, April 24, 2014. www.nytimes.com.
73. David Samadi, "E-Cigarettes May Be Causing New Health Risks, and Increased Vaping Among Teens Troubles Me," *New York Daily News*, July 17, 2015. www.nydailynews.com.
74. Editor, "Nine E-Juice Flavors That Sound Just like Kids' Favorite Treats," *Tobacco Unfiltered* (blog), Campaign for Tobacco-Free Kids, June 11, 2014. www.tobaccofreekids.org.
75. Jackler, "5 Questions."
76. Quoted in Reuters, "90% of 2,506 Doctors Think E-Cigarette Advertising Should Be Restricted," January 13, 2016. www.reuters.com.
77. Food and Drug Administration, "Proposed Rules," *Federal Register*, April 25, 2014. www.fda.gov.
78. William G. Shadel, Joan Tucker, and Steven Martino, "FDA's New Tobacco Rules Go Far Enough—for Now," *Hill*, June 12, 2014. http://thehill.com.
79. Quoted in Liz Szabo, "States Racing to Regulate E-Cigarettes," *USA Today*, February 7, 2015. www.usatoday.com.
80. C.S. Mott Children's Hospital, "Teens and Parents Agree: Place Restrictions on E-Cigarettes," 2015. http://mottnpch.org.
81. Gregory Conley, "Use Common Sense on E-Cigarettes," *U.S. News & World Report*, July 30, 2014. www.usnews.com.

82. Sean Gore, participant in *PBS NewsHour*, "Does Vaping Save Smokers or Create New Nicotine Addicts?," May 6, 2015. www.pbs.org.

83. Quoted in Erickson, "Boom in E-Cigarettes Sparks Call for Regulation."

84. Matthew Myers, participant in PBS NewsHour, "Does Vaping Save Smokers or Create New Nicotine Addicts?," May 6, 2015. www.pbs.org.

85. Michael Siegel, "National Survey Confirms That FDA E-Cigarette Regulations Would Renormalize Smoking," *The Rest of the Story: Tobacco News Analysis and Commentary* (blog), January 7, 2016. http://tobaccoanalysis.blogspot.com.

86. Siegel, "National Survey Confirms That FDA E-Cigarette Regulations Would Renormalize Smoking."

## Action on Smoking and Health (ASH)

701 Fourth St. NW
Washington, DC 20001
phone: (202) 659-4310 • fax (202) 289-7166
e-mail: info@ash.org • website: www.ash.org

ASH is an antismoking organization that seeks to educate the public about the risks of smoking and campaigns for tougher restrictions on cigarette and tobacco sales. Its website offers a number of articles and fact sheets about e-cigarettes and vaping.

## American Lung Association

55 W. Wacker Dr., Suite 1150
Chicago, IL 60601
phone: (800) 586-4872 • fax: (202) 452-1805
website: www.lung.org

The American Lung Association is the United States' leading source for lung health education and lung disease research, support, services, and advocacy. The website's search engine produces numerous publications about e-cigarettes, including statistical information.

## American Vaping Association (AVA)

736 Washington St.
Hoboken, NJ 07030
phone: (609) 947-8059
website: www.vaping.info

The AVA is a nonprofit organization that advocates for small- and medium-sized businesses in the vaping and e-cigarette industry. Its website offers news articles, testimonials, press releases, and a link to the AVA blog.

# Campaign for Tobacco-Free Kids

1400 I St. NW, Suite 1200
Washington, DC 20005
phone: (202) 296-5469 • fax: (202) 296-5427
website: www.tobaccofreekids.org

The Campaign for Tobacco-Free Kids advocates for policies that prevent kids from smoking, help smokers quit, and protect the public from secondhand smoke. Its website offers a large variety of materials about the effects of smoking, including numerous articles and fact sheets about e-cigarettes.

# Centers for Disease Control and Prevention (CDC)

1600 Clifton Rd.
Atlanta, GA 30329
phone: (800) 232-4636
website: www.cdc.gov

America's leading health protection agency, the CDC seeks to promote health and quality of life by controlling disease, injury, and disability. Its website's search engine produces a variety of articles and fact sheets about e-cigarette use among teens and adults.

# Consumer Advocates for Smoke-Free Alternatives Association (CASAA)

PO Box 652
Wilbraham, MA 01095
phone: (202) 241-9117
website: www.casaa.org

CASAA is an advocacy group that seeks to protect people's rights to access e-cigarettes and other vaping products. Its website offers fact sheets, testimonials, frequently asked questions, and a link to the CASAA news blog.

# Medical Organizations Supporting Vaping and Electronic Cigarettes (M.O.V.E.)

e-mail: efvispain.info@gmail.com
website: www.moveorganization.org

Developed by a group of vapers, M.O.V.E. seeks to educate the public and health professionals about the importance of e-cigarettes as harm-reduction tools that can save lives. Its website offers news articles and links to fact sheets and e-cigarette research.

# National Institute on Drug Abuse (NIDA)

National Institutes of Health
6001 Executive Blvd., Room 5213
Bethesda, MD 20892-9561
phone: (301) 443-1124
e-mail: information@nida.nih.gov • website: www.drugabuse.gov

NIDA supports research efforts and ensures the rapid dissemination of research to improve drug abuse prevention, treatment, and policy. The website offers a wealth of information about substance use and abuse, including fact sheets and articles about e-cigarettes.

# Office of Adolescent Health (OAH)

1101 Wootton Pkwy., Suite 700
Rockville, MD 20852
phone: (240) 453-2846
e-mail: oah.gov@hhs.gov • website: www.hhs.gov/ash/oah

An agency of the US Department of Health and Human Services, the OAH is dedicated to improving the health and well-being of adolescents. Its website offers information about teen substance abuse, including articles about e-cigarettes and vaping.

# Partnership for Drug-Free Kids

352 Park Ave. S., 9th Floor
New York, NY 10010
phone: (212) 922-1560 • fax: (212) 922-1570
website: www.drugfree.org

The Partnership for Drug-Free Kids is dedicated to helping parents and families solve the teenage substance abuse problem. Its website offers research findings, news articles, statistics, and fact sheets about e-cigarettes.

# FOR FURTHER RESEARCH

## Books

Elissa Bass, *E-Cigarettes: The Risks of Addictive Nicotine and Toxic Chemicals*. New York: Cavendish Square, 2016.

Christine Wilcox, *Thinking Critically: E-Cigarettes and Vaping*. San Diego, CA: ReferencePoint, 2016.

## Internet Sources

Jonathan Adler et al., "Bootleggers, Baptists, and E-Cigs," *Regulation*, Spring 2015. http://object.cato.org/sites/cato.org/files/serials/files/regulation/2015/3/regulation-v38n1-3.pdf.

Simon Akam, "Big Tobacco Fights Back: How the Cigarette Kings Bought the Vaping Industry," *Newsweek*, May 27, 2015. http://europe.newsweek.com/big-tobacco-fights-back-how-cigarette-kings-bought-vaping-industry-327758.

Michael Blanding and Madeline Drexler, "The E-Cig Quandary," *Harvard Public Health*, Spring 2015. www.hsph.harvard.edu/magazine-features/e-cigarette-quandary.

Steven Greenhut, "E-Cigs Under Fire, Despite Likely Benefits," *Reason*, February 20, 2015. https://reason.com/archives/2015/02/20/e-cigs-under-fire-despite-likely-benefit.

Sasha Keenan, Dyamond Jones, and Elise Martin, "What Teens Don't Know About E-Cigarettes Could Hurt Them," *Raleigh (NC) News & Observer*, September 28, 2015. www.newsobserver.com/living/health-fitness/article36815598.html.

Sandee LaMotte, "Where We Stand Now: E-Cigarettes," CNN, January 25, 2016. www.cnn.com/2015/12/31/health/where-we-stand-now-e-cigarettes.

Janet Raloff, "E-Cigarettes Proving to Be a Danger to Teens," *Science News*, June 30, 2015. www.sciencenews.org/article/e -cigarettes-proving-be-danger-teens.

Sara Rimer, "Behind the Vapor," *BU Today* (Boston University), October 20, 2014. www.bu.edu/research/articles/behind-the-vapor.

Christine Rushton, "Teens Find a New Use for E-Cigarettes: Vaping Marijuana," *USA Today*, September 7, 2015. www.usatoday .com/story/news/2015/09/04/e-cigarettes-vape-marijuana -students-connecticut/71703472/#.

Raquel Rutledge, "Lab Tests Reveal Popular E-Cigarette Liquids Contain Harmful Chemicals," *Milwaukee Journal Sentinel*, October 20, 2015. www.jsonline.com/watchdog/watchdogreports /lab-tests-reveal-popular-e-cigarette-liquids-contain-harmful -chemicals-b99583582z1-334833961.html.

Dean E. Schraufnagel, "Electronic Cigarettes: Vulnerability of Youth," *Pediatric Allergy, Immunology, and Pulmonology*, March 2015. www.ncbi.nlm.nih.gov/pmc/articles/PMC4359356/pdf/ped .2015.0490.pdf.

Celia Shatzman, "Everything You Need to Know About E-Cigarettes," *Teen Vogue*, February 4, 2014. www.teenvogue.com /story/e-cigarettes.

## Websites

**NIDA for Teens** (https://teens.drugabuse.gov). A product of NIDA, this site is especially designed for teens. It offers a great deal of information about alcohol, drugs, tobacco, and e-cigarettes.

**Student Science** (https://student.societyforscience.org/science news-students). This site is designed especially for teens and covers a wide variety of health- and science-related topics. Its search engine links to a number of articles about e-cigarettes and vaping.

**Teens Health** (http://teenshealth.org). Teens will find a wealth of information about health-related topics on this site, including articles about e-cigarettes and vaping.

*Note: Boldface page numbers indicate illustrations.*

Abrams, David B., 55
acetylcholine, 31
   receptor for, **32**
addiction
   brain chemistry and, 30–31
   to e-cigarettes, 38–39
   nicotine, 28
   potential for, of cigarettes *vs.*
      e-cigarettes, 35–36
   teens and risk of, 45
advertising/marketing, 52–53, **58**
   FDA regulation and, 56
Alexander, James, 43
Allen, Joseph, 25
American Academy of Child &
   Adolescent Psychiatry, 44
American Association of Poison
   Control Centers (AAPCC), 26
American Heart Association, 16
American Lung Association, 25
Anderson, Cameron, 40
Angst, Sarah, 10

Baeyens, Frank, 11
bath salts, 50
Belchetz, Brett, 18, 53
Beveridge, Roy A., 28
Bixby, Ryan, 61
Blendon, Robert, 16
brain
   addiction and, 30–31
   developing, nicotine and, 44–45
   nicotine addiction and, 30–31
bronchiolitis obliterans ("popcorn lung
   disease"), 23–24
Bullen, Chris, 12–13
Bures, Frank, 28
Burhenne, Mark, 27

Campaign for Tobacco-Free Kids, 52,
   56, 61
cancer, risk of, 22–23
Cantrell, Lee, 26
Castagna, Ron, 49
cathinones, synthetic, 50
Centers for Disease Control and
   Prevention (CDC), 8, 9, 13–14, 47
*Chemical & Engineering News* (trade
   journal), 6
cigalikes, 6
cigarettes/cigarette smoking, **13**, **37**
   addictiveness of, e-cigarettes *vs.*,
      35–36
   use of e-cigarettes as means of
      quitting, 9, 11–12, 13, 63
Cloud Nine, 50
Conley, Gregory, 14, 21–22, 60

diacetyl, 23–25
dopamine, 32–33
Dorff, Stephen, 52
Dunn, John, 29
Dutra, Lauren, 46

e-cigarettes/vaping products, **5**, **13**,
   **21**, **34**
   addictiveness of, cigarettes *vs.*,
      35–36
   advertising of, 52–53, **58**
   cancer risk of, 22–23
   challenges of quitting, 37–39
   debate over regulation of, 60–61
   FDA regulation of, 52–55
   first prototype for, 7
   as gateway to smoking, 45–48
   inventor of, 4
   as means of quitting smoking, 9,
      11–12, 13, 63
   online sales of, 55

percentage of US adults using, by
   smoking status, **9**
size of US market for, 7
uncertainty about, 15
e-liquids, **21**, **34**
   additives in, 20, 36
   dangers of concentrated nicotine in,
      26–27
   FDA regulation of, 54–55
   measurement of nicotine in, 34
   research on vapors from, 20–21
Erickson, Britt E., 6
Etter, Jean-François, 12

Family Smoking Prevention and
   Tobacco Control Act (2009), 53
FDA. *See* Food and Drug
   Administration, US
flakka, 50
flavorings, 6, 15, 20
   advertising targeting youth and,
      55–56
   diacetyl, 23–25
   opinion on banning vapor products
      with, 16
Food and Drug Administration, US
   (FDA), 8, 63
   objections to regulation by, 60–61
   regulation of e-cigarettes by, 52–55
formaldehyde, 20–21
Foulds, Jonathan, 20, 35
Franklin, Hayley, 49–50
Frieden, Thomas R., 14, 44–45
functional magnetic resonance
   imaging (fMRI), 38

Gilbert, Herbert A., 7
Girgis, Linda, 56
Goniewicz, Maciej, 33
Gore, Sean, 60–61
Green, Nick, 29–30
Grier, Jacob, 17

Harvard T.H. Chan School of Public
   Health, 16, 25
*Health Affairs* (journal), 53–54
Herzog, Bonnie, 7
Hon Lik, 4, 6, 7

Jackler, Robert, 12, 46, 56

K2, 50
Krishnan-Sarin, Suchitra, 15, 43
KU Leuven, 11

Lloyd, Rachael, 29
lungs
   diacetyl and, 23–24
   vapor and, 19–22

marijuana, vaping of, 49–50, 51
Marquette University, 25
Martino, Steven, 57–58
McConnell, Matt, 34
Miech, Richard, 42
*Milwaukee Journal Sentinel*
   (newspaper), 25
Monitoring the Future (MTF) survey, 40,
   41–42, 45–46
Morean, Meghan E., 49
Morgan, Mike, 34–35
Musick, Kaylee, 51
Myers, Matthew, 61

National Institute for Occupational
   Safety and Health, 24
National Institute on Drug Abuse
   (NIDA), 8, 31–32, 40
National Public Radio, 59
National Youth Tobacco Survey
   (Centers for Disease Control and
   Prevention), 13–14
N-Bomb, 50
neurons (nerve cells), 31
neurotransmitters, 31–33
*New England Journal of Medicine*, 20
Newsome, Debra, 50
*Nicotiana tabacum* (tobacco), 6
nicotine, 6, 48
   addictive nature of, 28
   brain chemistry and, 31–33
   brain development and, 44–45
   concentrated, in e-liquids, 26–27
   measurement of, in e-liquids, 34
   oral health and, 27
   problems with labeling content of, 33
   types of, in e-liquids, 35–36

opinion polls. *See* surveys

Peyton, David, 21
*Philadelphia Weekly* (newspaper), 52
poisonings, nicotine, from e-liquids, 26–27
polls. *See* surveys
"popcorn lung disease" (bronchiolitis obliterans), 24
pyrazines, 36

Rankin, K. Vendrell, 45
regulation, of vapor products
    by FDA, 52–58
    online sale of, 57
    by states, 58–59
Reinhardt, Skyler, 33
RTI International, 20
Ruyan company, 6

Samadi, David, 55
Schick, Suzaynn, 25–26
secondhand vapor, 25–26
Shadel, William G., 57–58
Siegel, Michael, 11, 43, 62, 63
smoking. *See* cigarettes/cigarette smoking
smoking cessation
    effectiveness of e-cigarettes for, 13
    use of e-cigarettes as means of, 9, 11–12, 13, 63
Spice, 50
Spira, Avrum, 19, 20, 22–23
Stadtmiller, Mandy, 38–39
surveys
    on addiction to e-smoking, 28–29
    on likelihood of vaping teens to try cigarettes, 46–47
    on prevalence of marijuana vaping, 49

on prevalence of tobacco/e-cigarettes among youth, 13–14, **47**
on reasons teens vape, 40–43
on regulation of e-cigarettes, 59
on safety of e-cigarettes, 16
of teens on risks of vaping, 42
on trying to quit e-smoking, 37–38
on use of e-cigarettes as means of quitting smoking, 9, 12, 63
on youth smoking rates, 45–46
synthetic drugs, 50

tetrahydrocannabinol (THC), 49
*Tobacco Control* (journal), 36
tobacco farming, e-cigarettes as boost for, 10
Tucker, Joan, 57–58

University of Hawaii, 46
University of Southern California, 42

vape mods, 6
vaping, **18**, **48**, **60**
    of marijuana, 49–50, 51
    of synthetic drugs, 50
vaping products. *See* e-cigarettes/vaping products
vaping tricks, 15, 43
*Vaporizing Times* (online trade publication), 10
Volkow, Nora D., 30, 44

Wagstaff, Keith, 5
Wall, Matt, 38
World Lung Foundation, 8

Yale University School of Medicine, 14–15

Zeller, Mitch, 15

# PICTURE CREDITS